LANDMARKS

EIGHTEEN WONDERS OF
THE NEW YORK WORLD

For Sally Simmons

Carl Spielvogel

Dr. Peter A. D. Rubin

Ian Jackson Arthur Carter

LANDMARKS
EIGHTEEN WONDERS OF
THE NEW YORK WORLD

BARBARALEE DIAMONSTEIN

Illustrations by Albert Lorenz

Harry N. Abrams, Inc., Publishers, New York

Page 1: Brooklyn Bridge
Pages 2-3: The Continents, *U.S. Custom House*
Page 5: Sculpture crowning the main facade,
Grand Central Terminal

EDITOR: Eric Himmel
DESIGNER: Joan Lockhart

Library of Congress Cataloging-in-Publication Data
Diamonstein, Barbaralee.
Landmarks : eighteen wonders of the New York world /
Barbaralee Diamonstein ; illustrations by Albert Lorenz.
p. cm.
Includes index.
Summary: Explores the architecture of New York City by examining
eighteen landmarks and discussing how and why they were built.
ISBN 0–8109–3565–1
1. Architecture—New York (N.Y.)—Juvenile literature.
2. Historic buildings—New York (N.Y.)—Juvenile literature.
3. Architecture and society—New York (N.Y.)—Juvenile literature.
4. New York (N.Y.)—Buildings, structures, etc.—Juvenile literature.
[1. Architecture—New York (N.Y.) 2. New York (N.Y.)—
Buildings, structures, etc.]
I. Lorenz, Albert, 1941–   ill. II. Title.
NA735.N5D5   1992
720′.9747′ 1—dc20   92–6164
CIP
AC

Published in 1992 by Harry N. Abrams, Incorporated, New York
A Times Mirror Company

Printed and bound in Japan

Contents

What Is a Landmark?

Have you ever thought about why things from the past attract our attention? An antique mechanical bank, for example, with a **cast-iron** figure of Uncle Sam who drops a coin into his tall striped hat when you press a lever, or a stately Model T Ford slowly rolling by on a busy highway, fill most people with curiosity. Who can resist playing with such toys or pausing to look at those cars as they pass?

Old things intrigue us: we want to know how they were constructed and how they were used. They mirror the present by helping us to understand how life was different in the past. Consider the manual typewriter, which is now seldom used. Compared with a new personal computer, it is a cumbersome machine. But imagine how convenient (and how liberating) even the simplest typewriter was to a secretary who had been accustomed to writing letters longhand, using a quill pen and bottle of ink— and some even had to make their own ink! The mechanical simplicity of a typewriter may even have certain advantages—it doesn't require electricity to operate and, with few delicate parts, it is more durable than a computer. Although we prefer not to live in a world that uses only manual typewriters, neither would we want to live in a world that doesn't make an effort to preserve some old ones—the best-designed or most unusual ones. (You can find some of the finest examples in New York's Museum of Modern Art Design Collection.)

There is a little bit of history in everything around us: furniture, clothing, toys, books, cars, music, buildings. And there are people who work to preserve the best examples of each of these. In cities, towns, and the countryside, there are buildings and places that are special because of their beauty or history, and they are referred to as landmarks.

Buildings are designated as landmarks because they have a distinctive style of architecture and a significant history. A landmark may be many things: a bridge, apartment building, house, skyscraper, store, hotel, theater, library, museum, church or synagogue, park, restaurant, or fence. In New York City, there are even *trees* that have been designated as landmarks, and in this book you will read about one of them. While it hasn't been fabricated, this particular tree has a history of its own, beginning with the man who planted it. When you step into most buildings—your home, your school, a movie theater, a museum, or even a train, bus, or subway station—you are entering a place that has a past, a history. Clearly, buildings play a very important part of life's events, and people will always remember, often with strong feelings, their school buildings or the place where they were born, got married, had fun, or had their children. You might think of landmarks as places that have strong associations for almost everyone. Every landmark has a different story to tell—a story that weaves together the arts of architecture, design, engineering, and invention; the lives of people; and events in our society. This book tells the story of eighteen landmarks in New York City.

Landmarks are often threatened with deterioration or destruction, from either neglect or the actions of people who wish to demolish them and replace them with new buildings. Do you think it is important that we try to preserve

Lion,

The New York

Public Library

landmarks? Do you think landmarks help to create a more livable, interesting, and memorable city? New York City *does* believe in preserving landmarks, and it reinforces that belief with an effective landmarks law.

Architectural landmarks help us appreciate building styles and construction methods. For example, the tall, soaring, and shiny Chrysler Building (see pages 124–31), built in 1928–30, is an excellent example of skyscraper construction and of the sleek **Art Deco Style.** More than that, the Chrysler Building has become a symbol of a time and place that people look upon with pride and even affection. When we see the **spire** of the Chrysler Building lit up at night, we are reminded of New York's worldwide reputation as a great, modern metropolis.

Historical landmarks are places where important events in American history occurred. New York's City Hall (see pages 30–37) has been the headquarters of the city government continuously since it was completed in 1812, and many important decisions regarding the city's future, decisions that shaped its development and growth, have been made there. City Hall would be noteworthy as an example of **Federal Style** architecture even if it had no historical associations, and significant as one of the most important commissions of America's first native-born architect, John McComb, Jr., who collaborated on the design with the French-born architect Joseph-François Mangin.

Sometimes, buildings survive because of their historical associations. For example, Bowne House (see pages 12–21) was probably not very different from hundreds of other farmhouses in the Northeast in the seventeenth century. Few remain, making those that do very precious. To discover the historical events that make the Bowne House memorable, you will want to read the first chapter of this book.

Cultural landmarks are places of artistic or social importance, such as concert halls, art museums, theaters, or places where distinguished or celebrated persons lived. The Metropolitan Museum of Art (see pages 72–85) opened in 1872 in a small row house and moved to its present location in Central Park in 1880. It is a complex that was built to house, protect, and make available to the public for both education and enjoyment one of the world's largest and finest collections of art. It includes examples of painting, sculpture, architecture, and the decorative arts from many cultures. The Theodore Roosevelt Birthplace National Historic Site (see pages 38–45) is, in comparison to the museum, a very modest and rather typical example of New York architecture, but it opens a window into the world of one of America's greatest heroes and the period in which he lived.

Who determines what is a landmark? In New York City, the Landmarks Preservation Commission, an agency of the New York City government, is responsible for identifying and designating (naming) and regulating landmarks. The commission consists of eleven commissioners, among them architects, concerned citizens, historians, city planners, a landscape architect, an interior designer, and a realtor. At least one resident from each of the five boroughs of New York City must be represented on the commission. Ten of the commissioners serve part-time on a volunteer basis; the eleventh is the chairperson, who is a full-time, paid commissioner. The commissioners are appointed for three-year terms by the mayor, who

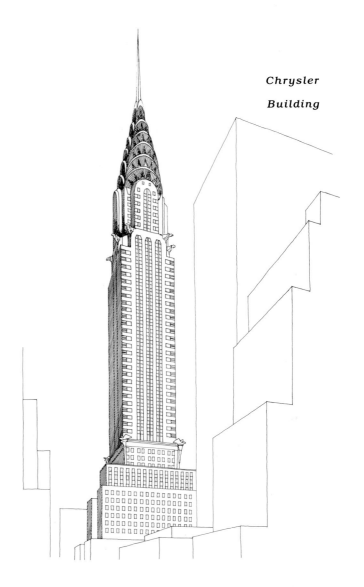

Chrysler Building

also selects the chairperson.

The commissioners set guidelines and policies for designation, and they meet at least twice a month to review, analyze, and eventually vote on designating landmarks. The commissioners also review applications from building owners who wish to make changes to designated properties. The commissioners determine if the proposed changes are appropriate to a specific building or to a historic district.

The meetings of the Landmarks Preservation Commission are public forums, where you and other citizens can voice opinions about the issues being considered and help influence the decisions being made. The commissioners work with a staff of architects, architectural historians, restoration specialists, planners, archaeologists, lawyers, and community groups, who help research and determine whether proposed sites should be designated, or whether proposed changes to already designated landmarks are appropriate.

When a New York City building is officially designated a landmark, it is protected by law. The building may not be torn down, or altered, without the prior approval of the New York City Landmarks Preservation Commission. If the owner wishes to make repairs or alterations to the building that would change its exterior, the plans must first be reviewed, and approved, by the commission. Concerned citizens and representatives of community groups, as well as design professionals, architects, lawyers, and government officials attend the public hearings of the Landmarks Preservation Commission. Through the public hearings, the building's owner as well as the public can let the commission know what they believe is best for their community. When concerned citizens speak out, they can help save important places from destruction as well as enhance a neighborhood for residents and visitors, too.

We are a society that tends to live continually in the present. Have you ever noticed how often people greet each other by saying, "What's new?" And it's not just an empty greeting. It has only been during the last thirty years or so that we have developed a greater regard for living in harmony with the past. In fact, it wasn't until 1965 that the New York City Landmarks Preservation Commission was formed, in the same year that the Landmarks Preservation Law was passed by the New York City government. At that time, New Yorkers began to feel a greater need to preserve beautiful buildings and unique places. Before then, as new construction took place all around the city, old buildings could be destroyed by their owners to make room for new ones without regard for their historic value or public discussion of the consequences. Many people felt that some special places should have been saved. Once the Landmarks Preservation Law was passed, old buildings could be protected. It is thanks, in large measure, to the Landmarks Preservation Law that we still have many of the city's architectural treasures, some of which you will read about in this book.

Landmarks can be many things. In New York City, there are four different types of landmarks:

- Individual landmarks, where the exterior of a building is designated.
- Interior landmarks, where the inside of a building to which the public has access is designated.
- Scenic landmarks, which are not buildings. These include bridges, parks, water towers, piers, cemeteries, sidewalk clocks, fences, and even trees.
- Historic districts, which are entire areas that have architectural unity and quality. A historic district is protected under the landmarks law because it represents a period or style of architecture that is typical of an era in the city's history. All of the buildings within a historic district are then protected by the landmarks law, and only changes that are appropriate to the district can be made in that area. The largest historic districts include Greenwich Vil-

lage, the Upper East Side, and the Upper West Side in Manhattan, and Brooklyn Heights, all of which encompass many blocks. The smallest historic districts, such as Hunters Point in Queens, are only a block or part of a block. Most historic districts, such as Longwood in the Bronx, are small enclaves of residential or commercial buildings, covering all or part of three to five city blocks.

In the past twenty-seven years, the Landmarks Preservation Commission has been successful in designating a large number of places in the city. Since its formation in 1965, the commission has designated 910 individual landmarks, 85 interior landmarks, 9 scenic landmarks, and 55 historic districts and 6 extensions of historic districts. While that may seem like a great number to you, it is still less than 2 percent of all the building lots in the five boroughs of New York City.

This book will help you explore some of New York City's most interesting and significant places. You can learn a lot about history through the story of a building and the people who designed, built, and lived or worked in it.

As you travel around the city, look at all the different kinds and styles of buildings that have survived. What do you think New York City will look like in the future? It is hard to tell. Perhaps in thirty years places that seem brandnew to us now, and that might not seem worth preserving, will be landmarks, examples of styles from the past that people find they appreciate when they are no longer commonplace.

Does the city or town in which you live have a landmarks law? Do you think a landmarks law is a good thing for a community, large or small? As we move toward a more balanced and thoughtful use of our environment, more and more people have come to realize that for a place to have meaning, to be worth living in, there is a need to feel some connection to, and regard for, what came before.

Finally, a few words about how to use this book. Throughout its pages, you will find words printed in **boldface** type. These words are defined in the glossary at the end of the book. All of the buildings included are open to the public at varying times—some as museums and others simply as public buildings—except The Dakota. If you are making a special trip to visit any of the buildings you should telephone in advance.

Bowne House

1 6 6 1

Weeping Beech

1 8 4 7

There are very few seventeenth-century houses remaining in the United States; in fact, there are few remaining in all of North America. In the 1600s, almost all modest residences were built of wood, which is the least permanent of building materials. The oldest surviving house in New York City, the Pieter Claesen Wyckoff House at Clarendon Road and Ralph Avenue in Brooklyn (which is also a des-ignated landmark), was built in 1641, less than twenty years after the first European settlement of what was then called New Amsterdam. Almost as old, and the oldest house in Queens, is the Bowne House, 37–01 Bowne Street, of 1661. Often, buildings are preserved because of some historic event with which they are associated. This is certainly true of Bowne House, but it may also owe its survival to the

Bowne House

fact that nine generations of the Bowne family lived in the house, from 1661 to 1945!

Colonial America lured people for whom the worship of their God defined the way they lived, their social habits, their education, even the clothes they wore and almost every other aspect of life. Although many early settlers immigrated to America to escape religious persecution in the Old World, they soon found a lack of tolerance in the New World as well. Religious freedom, or "freedom of conscience," as they called it—which was the right of a person to exercise his or her own judgment in matters

of religion—was won through the efforts and perseverance of numerous individuals. One of them was John Bowne, an Englishman, who in 1649 adopted America as his new home, and who helped pave the way for religious freedom and democracy.

John Bowne was born in Derbyshire, England, in 1627. At the age of twenty-two, he emigrated to America with his family. Along with many other English people, they were seeking to establish a different life for themselves in America. Among the earliest settlements in the Dutch **colony** of New Netherland

The 1695 extension

(later renamed New York) was the town of Vlissingen, first settled in 1642 and named after a town in Flanders; it is now known as Flushing. It was here, in 1651, that the Bowne family chose to settle permanently and farm, after spending two years in the Massachusetts Bay Colony, where they first landed. In 1656, John Bowne married Hannah Feke, the stepdaughter of William Hallett, the sheriff of the town.

The Bowne family probably chose to settle in Flushing because John's sister Dorothy was betrothed to Edward Farthington of Flushing. It is possible that John Bowne read a popular pamphlet in which Long Island was referred to as ideal for farming, with fertile land and excellent harbors and bays.

Another reason why the family might have chosen this location as its new home was that on October 10, 1645, Governor William Kieft of New Netherland had granted the town a charter assuring freedom of religious worship to anyone who would settle and farm the land. While Governor Kieft was in office, the Dutch government guaranteed that Flushing would have no single established church to the exclusion of other religious groups. The governor hoped that the liberal attitude of the charter would attract immigrants, especially among those facing economic hardship and religious oppression in Puritan New England.

This evolving spirit of tolerance was nearly crushed when the unpopular Governor Peter Stuyvesant succeeded Governor Kieft in 1647. Stuyvesant's often overbearing loyalty to the Dutch Reformed Church, the established church of Holland, overshadowed his commitment to "liberty of conscience." His most serious violation of the original charter occurred in August of 1657, when he issued a ban ordering Flushing residents to avoid any "interaction" with a group of Quakers who had arrived in New Amsterdam from England in 1656 and settled in Flushing.

More than any other religious sect during the seventeenth century, the Quakers, who called themselves the Society of Friends, aroused great controversy, because of their relentless opposition to other Protestant sects, such as Congregationalists and Presbyterians. Their group was formed in England in 1645 by George Fox, who rejected organized churches because of what he saw as their inflexible doctrines. Quakers were inclined to preach in the streets and were even known to interrupt services in other churches in order to express their own beliefs. They were easily identified by the deliberate simplicity of their style of dress and manner. Their congregations in "meetinghouses" for worship were held without any organized service, and there was no single speaker appointed to lead the service. Their belief that all men were created equal led them to refuse to recognize civil or ecclesiastical authority. This staunch attitude was not always accepted by others around them, and it set off a wave of intolerance and persecution in the form of government fines and threats of imprisonment.

In 1657, Governor Stuyvesant issued a ban with the intention of suppressing the Quakers and anyone who showed them hospitality. A proclamation was issued, printed, and posted in every town, declaring that any person caught associating with Quakers would be fined and punished. On December 27, 1657, the townspeople of Flushing responded to the ban by issuing a remonstrance, a formal statement of their grievances, to the governor. This docu-

Front door

was preparing to raise his family in Flushing. Little did he realize that he and his house would soon play a role in events that would influence the growth of individual rights, and the evolution of democracy, in America. He did not even sign the remonstrance, although he must have been fully aware of the mounting turmoil in the community, since records show that he had become a Quaker by 1662.

That year, John Bowne defied Governor Stuyvesant's ban against the Quakers by permitting them to conduct religious meetings in his house. Until then, they had been conducting their meetings secretly, often at night in the hidden recesses of the woods. Word spread that Quakers were meeting in Bowne's house, and complaints were made by officials of the nearby town of Jamaica. As a result, an outraged Stuyvesant had Bowne arrested in September 1662. He was ordered to pay a fine and to discontinue his support of the Quakers. When Bowne refused to do either, he was placed in solitary confinement in a jail at the fort in New Amsterdam, with only coarse bread and water to sustain himself.

Even this punishment failed to sway Bowne from his convictions, and, after three months, on December 31, 1662, Governor Stuyvesant decided to banish him from the colony, forcing him to part with his wife and three young children. Stuyvesant might have thought twice about sending Bowne away for not paying his fine had he known what Bowne would do. Departing New Netherland on the ship *The Fox*, he landed in Ireland and made his way to Holland, where he petitioned the Dutch West India Company. He pled his case effectively, using in his own defense the written copy of the original charter granted by Governor Kieft,

ment, a customary way among the Dutch to express public opinion, was a two-page petition stating the intentions of the people of Flushing to allow the Quakers to reside and worship in the community.

Thirty-one residents of Flushing signed the Flushing Remonstrance, expressing their desire to uphold freedom of conscience for all of their neighbors and to protest Peter Stuyvesant's violation of their rights. In January of 1658, Sheriff Tobias Feake delivered the remonstrance to the governor. The document incited the governor's fury, and caused him to dismiss Sheriff Feake from office, imprison him, and fine three other town officials who had also signed it. At the same time, John Bowne which stated that all residents of Flushing were guaranteed liberty of conscience. After a hearing in Holland by a committee of the Amsterdam Chamber of the Dutch West India Company, he was released in January, 1664, and allowed to return home to Flushing. With him he brought a letter from the Dutch government directing Governor Stuyvesant to cease his persecution of the Quakers and to allow the residents of Flushing their rights.

It took John Bowne a full nineteen months to travel back to America and rejoin his family in Flushing. But the sacrifices that he and his family made for the sake of liberty were well rewarded with the cessation of religious persecution in the colony, establishing the fundamental principle of freedom of worship that is the heritage of all Americans.

Aside from its symbolic value in the history of America, Bowne House is also a fine example of early Colonial architecture, influenced by Dutch and English styles. The term *Colonial* refers to a relatively standardized system of architecture that emerged in America during the 1600s and lasted until the 1800s. This means that certain factors, such as climate, natural resources, and cultural inheritance, helped define the evolution of a widely accepted system of structure, **plan**, and decoration.

The early colonists were faced with a harsh and often hostile environment, seasonal extremes of heat and cold that they had rarely experienced in Europe, times of severe drought or flooding rain, as well as threats from Native American tribes who felt displaced from their homelands. Can you imagine the discomforts they must have faced in this undeveloped territory? The building of adequate shelters was one of their first tasks. The lack of money and effec-

tive building tools meant that simplicity and practicality were key factors in determining their style and method of building.

Since the colonists came from European countries that were highly developed economically and culturally, one might expect that their shelters would have been similarly sophisticated in design and construction. However, the lack of a labor force and of adequate tools meant that early settlers in North America had to live in small huts and crude dugouts. Records from January, 1608, claim that the relief ships sent to aid the colonists who landed in Jamestown, Virginia, on May 14, 1607, found them inhabiting primitive dwellings. It is not surprising that Massachusetts Governor William Bradford noted that nearly half the people who arrived in Plymouth Harbor on the *Mayflower* on December 16, 1620, died within two or three months of landing because of the harsh climate.

In New Amsterdam, the secretary of New Netherland described similar wretched living conditions of the first families in the 1620s. Their crude shelters consisted mainly of burrows formed by digging pits six to seven feet deep in the ground that were surrounded by wooden stakes driven into the earth and lashed together to form walls. The roofs were bark or **thatch**, a covering made of straw, rushes, or leaves, mixed with mud. Needless to say, these early lodgings provided insufficient defense against the wind, rain, and cold. Even the Bowne house may have had a thatch roof before they were banned in the 1640s because of the fire hazard they presented.

The urgent need for adequate shelter in America led the home countries to send skilled craftsmen, such as carpenters and masons, to aid the colonists. Furthermore, after the first difficult years of adjustment in the new land, the settlers began to discover its natural resources, such as wood, stone, **marble**, slate, sand, and clay. These ideal building materials made it possible for the colonists to develop a new form of architecture that adapted Western European styles to the needs of a rural, pioneer society.

Given this background, we can better understand and appreciate the features of Bowne House that define early Colonial architecture. Since simplicity and practicality were required of the early shelters, it is logical that they were based on examples of European rural structures, which were inherently modest and would have been familiar to the colonists, as opposed to the grandiose public buildings, cathedrals, and manors of **Gothic** Europe. As a result, both the interiors and exteriors of Colonial buildings were generally unadorned and unpretentious, and attempted to address the necessities of life in a pioneer society.

The dense forests of North America provided wood, which was versatile, easy to work with, and in abundance, making it the principal building material of the settlers. In his journal, John Bowne noted that he handpicked each white cedar and oak tree to be used in building his house during numerous strolls through the woods on his property. Since there was not yet a lumber industry to provide the settlers with quantities of sawed wood, every piece of wood had to be hand-hewn, making the building process slow and tedious. Although there are unauthenticated reports of early sawmills (in Maine in 1631, and in New Netherland in 1633) in which the wood would have been cut in an economical and mechanized manner, mill sawing was not widely employed until the appearance of steam power and the circular saw in the nineteenth century.

After cutting the wood, the next step in building was the construction of the house frame. The settlers preferred to use oak to form the massive **beams** that held up the walls and floors, because it was the sturdiest type of wood. (The extension Bowne built onto his house in 1680 still has its original oak floors.) To connect the beams, joints requiring skillful craftsmanship were prepared. Round wooden pegs, called *treenails*, were run through the fastened joints to secure them. This system preceded the use of machine-made nails, which were not available until the 1830s.

When the "skeleton" frame, which was usually made of oak and served as a primary support, was completed, the space was enclosed with walls and a roof. The most common exterior wall surface, or **siding**, was made of **clapboards**, which were thin, flat boards about five inches wide and about four to six feet long. The clapboards were tapered along one edge and nailed in horizontal rows, each overlapping by about an inch the one below it, to vertical timbers, called **studs**, which in turn were attached to the basic frame of the house. The walls were insulated with a filling that consisted of a mixture of clay, chopped straw, and animal hair. This **insulation**, called *cobbing*, is fifteen inches thick in some portions of the Bowne house. The hand-forged iron nails that were used to build the exterior walls were so highly valued that people collected and reused them whenever a house burnt down. They handed the nails down from one generation to another.

Although the building techniques and materials became standardized as time progressed, there was still considerable variety in seventeenth-century house plans. Since each house was usually built by its owner, the size and **layout** of the house were determined mostly by the size of the family, their financial circumstances, and the climate of the region.

The Bowne House in 1661 consisted of a large room, or hall, with a sleeping loft, which was the first type to appear among early Colonial houses. The front door opened into a small space, called the **porch** in those days, from which one entered the hall. This main room combined the functions of the kitchen, dining room, and living room, and had an enormous fireplace, or **hearth**, where the occupants of the house could find warmth, light, and comfort, and where they could share their meals, read, spin thread, cook, or do any other daily tasks. If there were too many people in the house, and not enough beds to sleep in, guests or members of the family would sleep in the hall. In fact, it was very often the most comfortable place to sleep, since the fireplace was the only source of heat during Colonial times.

The hearth of Bowne House was large and the fire was kept burning at all times. In the left-hand corner of the fireplace, a small hole in the shape of a half circle opened to what was called a **beehive oven**. This oven, for baking bread, was heated with wood embers from the fireplace; the dough was put in the hot oven after the embers were removed. It was at this hearth that John Bowne welcomed many guests, including the Quakers, to share his food and his ideas.

Illumination was yet another problem when living in a Colonial house. The scarcity of candles (the vast majority of early Americans had

to make them themselves) or oil for lamps meant that much of the house interior was dark. Windows of the earliest houses were few and very small—not more than a foot and a half squared. A number of considerations determined the size of the windows: the need to maintain warmth in the house in the winter, protection from Indian attacks, and most important, the scarcity and high cost of glass. Most of these windows were stationary, which

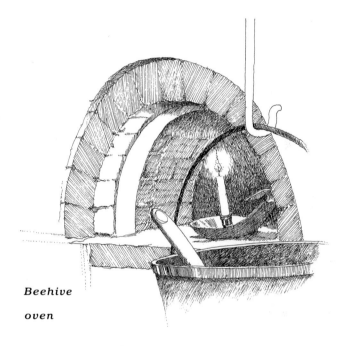

Beehive oven

meant that it was not possible to open them. To us today, this would feel very confining, but during the seventeenth and eighteenth centuries night air was thought to be poisonous, so windows that opened were not a necessity, or even considered desirable by many. Originally, the windows in the Bowne House may not have had glass in them, but there were shutters outside to help keep out the cold air.

One solution to the problem of ventilation and illumination was the **Dutch door**. Originating in Holland, this type of door was divided in half, so that the top and bottom could be opened and closed separately. During the day, the top half would be opened in order to allow the fresh air and sunlight in, while the closed bottom half kept animals out, and small children in.

Sometime after 1661, John Bowne added a second floor to his house, with two bedrooms. Their small size and low ceilings helped to ensure that they would retain heat better in the winter. Bedrooms in Colonial houses were always congested, since it was not uncommon for two or three people to sleep in one bed, and there was usually more than one bed in each room. **Trundle beds**—low beds that could be pushed under the larger ones when not in use—for children were often put in their elders' rooms, although the Bowne house probably did not have them. The most common type of bed had a canopy and muslin curtain to enclose the bed on all sides, to make it warmer at night.

In 1680, a dining room was added to Bowne House; and a year after John Bowne's death in 1695, an extension in the New England *saltbox* style was built, with a living room, or **parlor**, downstairs and more bedrooms upstairs. **Saltboxes**, or **lean-tos**, characteristically had a roof that started at the top of the house in front and ended close to the ground in back. They were called saltboxes because their shape actually resembled that of a salt box. Colonial wooden boxes were very specialized, with a different size and shape to hold every imaginable household item, such as tobacco, clay pipes, bread, candles, and of course salt.

The parlor, or living room, would have been the best room of the house, containing the most valued furniture, as well as treasured possessions. Here the family received guests, neighbors, and friends, and held important ceremonies, such as weddings and funerals. In the parlor of the Bowne House, the most notable feature is the unusually fine eighteenth-century wood paneling on the walls. Each panel is carved in a **cross-and-Bible pattern**, giving the walls linear definition and a sense of depth. Here there is a collection of **portraits** of various members of the Bowne family.

From 1661 to 1945, a total of nine generations of Bowne family descendants occupied the original home of John Bowne (who was married three times in the course of his life in Flushing). On October 10, 1945, the Bowne House was purchased by the Bowne House Historical Society, founded by Justice Charles C. Colden and John Bowne's direct descendants, Anna, Bertha, and William Parsons, to be preserved as a **shrine** to religious freedom in America. It was opened to the public on July 4, 1947, as a part of the festivities celebrating Independence Day.

Another aspect of the Bowne family legacy is a scenic landmark on Bowne Street, which stands near the house in the center of an adjacent playground. Located only two hundred feet east of the house, this landmark is a living one—the oldest tree of its kind in America—called the weeping beech tree. This remarkable tree is over sixty feet tall, with a trunk circumference of fourteen feet and a spread of eighty-five feet.

The weeping beech was planted in 1847 by Samuel Bowne Parsons, a direct descendant of John Bowne. The weeping beech tree was grown from a small shoot taken from a tree on the **estate** of Baron De Mann in Beersal, Belgium. The cutting was brought home in a flowerpot by Samuel Bowne Parsons himself.

Samuel Bowne Parson's mother, Mary

Weeping beech

Bowne, had inherited the Bowne House in 1831 and occupied the house with her husband, Samuel Parsons, a leader of the Society of Friends in New York City and a nurseryman. Samuel Parsons established a nursery in 1838 on land given to him by Mary's parents, where most of the playground is today. In this nursery, Parsons grew many species of trees and planted exotic varieties of plants from foreign countries that could survive in the local environment. (Flushing was then the nursery center of the United States and supplied trees to the rest of the country.)

The tree has successfully endured the years and the elements. During the spring and summer seasons, the dense foliage of the tree shades the floor of the playground, for visitors and residents of Flushing to enjoy.

Morris-Jumel

Mansion

Morris-Jumel Mansion

1765

In 1765, ten years before the American Revolution began, and over one hundred years after John Bowne moved to Flushing, New York was a city of about twenty thousand people. Almost all of the buildings were at the southern end of Manhattan Island, in what we now know as the Wall Street financial district. New York, like Massachusetts and Pennsylvania, was a British **colony**; its inhabitants were subjects of King George III of England.

After Boston, New York was the second-largest city in the colonies; a bustling cluster of town houses, taverns, churches, schools, and shops surrounded by miles of forest and farmland. It was also a busy port, where rich merchants traded beaver furs, lumber, tobacco,

22

whale oil, and flour. The city was expanding rapidly. Hundreds of new buildings went up each year, and some of the wealthier citizens sought to escape the crowding by building country houses in the northern part of the island.

During this prosperous time in the 1760s, Roger Morris, a British colonel, and his American wife, Mary Philipse Morris, built a **mansion** that they called Mount Morris on one of the highest hills in Manhattan, an area called Harlem Heights. This country house, now at 1765 Jumel Terrace, is Manhattan's only surviving house that was built before the Revolutionary War.

Imagine yourself on the **porch** of this splendid house, high on a hill. You would have been able to see out over the countryside in every direction from this spot: to the south, New York Harbor and Staten Island; to the north, the rolling hills of Westchester; to the east, the East River, Long Island Sound, and Connecticut; and to the west, the Hudson River and the jagged Palisades of New Jersey. What an impressive view this must have been from the large wooden house on its vast **estate** of rolling hills and country roads.

Colonel Roger Morris served in the British Army under General Edward Braddock and fought in the French and Indian Wars in the 1750s and early 1760s. During these wars, France and England fought over land in Canada and parts of the present-day northeastern United States, and the British forced the French out of North America. George Washington also served under General Braddock and knew Morris.

In 1758, Morris married Mary Philipse, who was a member of a wealthy family that owned thousands of acres of property along the Hudson River in Westchester County. An old farm, a manor house, and a few acres of their land are now the site of a museum called Philipsburg Manor, near Tarrytown, New York. In 1765, when Roger and Mary Morris built Mount Morris as their summer home, they already had a town house in lower Manhattan. Mount Morris must have been a welcome escape from the hot, crowded streets of the city (does that sound familiar?) to the cooler, scenic countryside. It was probably about a four-hour carriage ride from their town house to their country house.

The Morrises must have wanted the mansion to be a very special place, because its architecture is different from, and far more elaborate than, Colonial farmhouses like Bowne House (see pages 12–21). Colonel Morris was probably familiar with many interesting building designs because his father, also named Roger Morris, was an architect in England. Mount Morris is a typical example of **Georgian Style** architecture. In England, the style popular during the 1760s, when this house was built, was called Georgian, after King George III, the monarch who reigned then. Georgian architecture is based on the Palladian Style of the late Italian **Renaissance**, in which the design is **symmetrical** and uses **Classical orders**. That style is named for the man who created it. His name was Andrea Palladio, and he was an Italian architect who lived from 1508 to 1580.

The **floor plan** of the first floor of the mansion shows rooms of the same shape and dimension on either side of a central hallway. When you walk through the front door of the house, you can look all the way through to the very back wall. Nothing blocks your view because the stairway to the second floor is hidden off to the side of the hall. Doors to all of the rooms are situated off the long straight hallway. The rooms downstairs were for various social activities; as always in traditional houses, the upstairs rooms were bedrooms.

In the Morris-Jumel Mansion, the hallway leads to an octagonal **drawing room** at the back of the house. An octagon is an eight-sided shape, and the octagonal room has eight walls. This octagonal room was one of the first of its kind in American architecture. The drawing room was used for parties and dances. After

dinner, guests would withdraw from the dining room to another room where they could dance or relax. The term *drawing room* (what most people now call the living room) is probably a shortened version of "withdrawing room."

Besides the symmetrical **layout** of the rooms inside, another way to identify its Geor-

gian Style is by the combination of elements that make up the **facade** of the house. These include the tall **columns** in front of the building that support a triangular piece of the roof called a **pediment**. The columns, together with the pediment, create what is known as a **portico**—a great covered porch—at the front of the house. A portico is another design element that is often seen in Georgian Style buildings.

The Morris family lived in their mansion from 1765 until the Revolutionary War began in 1775. During the war Roger Morris and his family remained loyal to the British. Because the revolutionaries sometimes resorted to violence to force British loyalists to abandon their property, the Morrises felt that they could not safely remain in their house. So Roger Morris returned to his home in England, and his wife and children went to Mrs. Morris's family home, the Philipse estate in Yonkers, New York. Mount Morris remained empty for several months until General George Washington used the house as temporary headquarters for his American troops.

Washington stayed at Mount Morris from September 14 until October 20, 1776. The upstairs level of the octagonal room became his office, and court-martials to punish disloyal American soldiers were held in a white tent on the property. This was a dark time for the American forces, which were slowly retreating in the face of the advancing British army after their defeat in the Battle of Long Island (August 27), at Brooklyn Heights. While at the mansion, Washington successfully held off the British at the Battle of Harlem Heights (September 16), which was fought close to where Columbia University is now located, near

Octagonal drawing room

Broadway and 116th Street. Within a month, however, the British had gained control of the city, and Washington and his troops moved north to Westchester. Before they left, a terrible fire broke out downtown in the main part of the city, on September 28, 1776. It was thought that American patriots set fire to the city so that the British would not be able to stay there. Most of the city was destroyed, including the Morrises' town house.

After Washington and his troops departed, the mansion was used by British and German commanders until the Revolutionary War ended in 1783. At that time, the house and land were taken over by the American government. After the war, the property of British loyalists in America was often confiscated. As the Morris family had fled to England, the American government leased the Mount Morris land for farming. The house was sold to a private owner and became a tavern.

The tavern was called Calumet Hall; *calumet* is a Native American word for peace pipe, and the name was meant to convey the feeling that it was a friendly place to eat, or to stay overnight. The tavern was one of the first stops outside the city along the Albany Post Road, which led from New York all the way north to Albany—almost two hundred and fifty miles.

By 1790, George Washington had become the first president of the United States. Washington once stopped at the tavern for a dinner with the vice president, John Adams of Massachusetts (who succeeded Washington as president) and some members of his cabinet (and some of their wives), including Thomas Jefferson from Virginia, who was secretary of state and later the third president of the United States; Alexander Hamilton from New York,

who was secretary of the treasury; Henry Knox from Massachusetts, who was secretary of war; and James Madison from Virginia, an important member of Congress and later the fourth president of the United States. The tavern keeper certainly must have tried to prepare a delicious meal for such an important dinner. But can you imagine—everything they ate had to be cooked over a wood fire, in the large fireplace in the kitchen.

The kitchen is in the basement of the mansion, and in those days, as in other Colonial kitchens, the cooking was done at a large open **hearth**, or fireplace. The floor in front of the hearth was made of stone extending a few feet out into the room. An iron "arm" in the shape of a large hook that swung out over the logs of the fire was attached to the back of the fireplace wall. From this arm pots were hung by their handles over the heat. Many other pots and pans could be laid around the hearth to keep food warm. There was also an oven with a rounded side, called a **beehive oven**, set into the wall of the fireplace. This is where bread was baked, using some of the very hot wood embers from the fire to heat the oven. This simple arrangement must have worked well enough to cook a meal for the president and his party.

The days of the tavern did not last very long, however. A few years later the house was purchased by a wealthy couple named Stephen and Eliza Jumel. Jumel was a wine merchant from France; in 1804 he had married Eliza Bowen, who had grown up in Rhode Island. She was said to be both beautiful and brilliant—and rumored to be the illegitimate child of a prostitute. Although she was quite poor, she managed to educate herself, learned to speak French, and was able to charm the men of so-

Main facade with
Federal Style decoration

called high society with her worldly manners and opinions. Before she married Jumel, Eliza lived downtown in New York City and was friends with some of the important American political figures, including Aaron Burr and Thomas Jefferson. Despite her abilities, she was not always accepted by other people in New York society, though she was well known throughout her life because of her varied experiences, and her accumulation of enormous wealth.

When the Jumels moved into the Morris mansion in 1810, they made several changes so that the style of the house would be up-to-date. Buildings often reflect the fashion of the times, as well as serve as a personal expression of the

people who live in them. Each new resident of a place seeks a way to make it his or her own, whether it is the place where we work, live, play, shop, or learn. Think about some place that is your own—your desk at school, your bedroom, a favorite place to read or think or watch TV. How have you made this your own place? Does it say something about your style, taste, and values?

The changes the Jumels made to Mount Morris were in the **Federal Style**—a new style named after the federation of states that formed the United States. This was the first new architectural style of our newly independent country, and it was popular after the Revolution, from about 1790 until about 1840.

The most significant changes to the mansion, typical of the Federal Style, are those that were made to the front door. The Jumels installed a new door, with panels on either side containing stained-glass windows, called **sidelights**. Above the door, another window was installed, called a **fanlight**. A fanlight is a window with a semicircular top, shaped very much like a fan. The panes of glass are separated by leading that looks like the ribs of a fan or the spokes of a bicycle wheel. There are three lovely fanlight windows on the facade of the house. One is above the front door, another is above the door on the second floor, and the third is located in the triangular pediment and serves as a window for the attic.

The Jumels also redesigned the **balcony** above the front door, adding **balustrades**. There is a door in the second-floor hallway that opens onto the balcony. From there the view north must have been even more spectacular than from the portico. Balustrades were added to the roof as well. Balustrades are low, fence-like decorative elements that run along the edge of a balcony or the top of the roof. They are decorations that add to the overall elegance of the house. For the inside of the house, there were also new mahogany banisters on the stairs.

After about five years, the Jumels decided to return to France, where they were welcomed into French society. From 1816 to 1826, they traveled back and forth between their homes in Paris and New York. Because he was in serious financial trouble in France, Mr. Jumel transferred ownership of the Jumel mansion from himself to his adopted daughter. He assigned power of attorney to manage his affairs in the United States to his wife. This meant that Eliza Jumel now had access to property and money; in fact, she became a wealthy woman in her own right.

While they were in France, the Jumels were frequent visitors to Napoléon's court. Napoléon Bonaparte was the emperor of France from 1804 until 1814. During his reign, he established an important set of laws in France, called the Napoleonic Code, that helped modernize that country's legal system. Napoléon led the French army in several wars and conquered much of Europe; he wanted to rule the entire continent. Exiled to the island of Elba in the Mediterranean Sea by his enemies in 1814, he escaped and reclaimed his army, but he was decisively defeated by the combined forces of the English, Austrians, Prussians, and Russians at the Battle of Waterloo (June 18, 1815) in Belgium. At this time the Jumels offered to help Napoléon escape to the United States, but he surrendered and spent the rest of his life in exile on Saint Helena, a British island west of southern Africa. Despite his defeat, the Jumels must have thought of Napoléon as a brilliant hero—their offer of safe passage was considered a brave gesture.

By 1826, Mrs. Jumel had returned to America permanently, and she brought many pieces of furniture back with her from France, as well as nearly one hundred paintings, which was the largest collection of art in New York up to that time. Some of the furniture, including a mahogany bed that is now exhibited in the house, had belonged to Napoléon. Mrs. Jumel redecorated the house in the **Empire Style**, which was created in France in the early years of Napoléon's reign. This style was formal, elaborate, and very decorative, often using figured mahogany and either gold or brass ornamentation.

In 1832, Stephen Jumel died of injuries he

received in a carriage accident. Eliza Jumel inherited his fortune, and became one of the wealthiest women in New York. One year later, she renewed her friendship with, and then married, the former vice president of the United States, Aaron Burr. The wedding took place in the front **parlor** of the mansion in July 1833. Burr was seventy-seven years old and Mrs. Jumel was fifty-nine.

Aaron Burr was a colorful, and controversial, figure. He had served in the Revolutionary Army, and later became vice president to Thomas Jefferson. He was notorious for his 1804 duel with Alexander Hamilton. Hamilton had served as secretary of the treasury under President Washington. Hamilton and Burr had a long-standing disagreement about how to structure the country's banking system: Hamilton favored a national bank, but Burr preferred a state-by-state system. Because of this disagreement, they became political rivals, and personal rivals as well. After an argument (no one is quite sure what it was about), Burr challenged Hamilton to a duel, which was held on the Weehawken Heights, New Jersey. Hamilton was wounded and died a few days later.

Like Mrs. Jumel, Burr had lived briefly in Europe before their marriage. He had gone there after being tried and acquitted for conspiring to conquer territory in the Southwest and Mexico for his own aggrandizement. By the time Burr and Eliza Jumel were married, he was a lawyer in New York City. It was said that Burr used Eliza's money to **speculate** in Texas real estate, and that much of it was lost. After six months the marriage ended, and in 1836 they were officially divorced, a few months before Burr died.

Mrs. Jumel continued to divide her time between her town house in lower Manhattan, the Harlem Heights mansion, and her home upstate in Saratoga Springs. In the last few years before her death in 1865 at the age of ninety-one, she lived alone in the mansion, and it is said that she was lonely and eccentric.

After Eliza Jumel died, there were many disputes among her relatives about who would inherit the house. Mrs. Jumel had left her entire fortune to a variety of charities rather than to family members. Eventually, in 1882, her nephew by marriage, Nelson Chase, and his daughter, Eliza Jumel Chase, inherited the house. Five years later, Chase sold the property. Between 1887 and 1903 the property was bought and sold many times.

The last private owners were General Ferdinand Pinney Earle and his wife, Lillie. In 1903, after the general died, Mrs. Earle persuaded New York City to buy the property in order to preserve it as a place of historical importance. An organization now called the Morris-Jumel Mansion, Inc., was formed to maintain the interior of the house and help visitors learn about its history.

The original house is now a museum, called the Morris-Jumel Mansion after its two principal owners. New York City owns the property and the New York City Department of Parks and Recreation maintains it. Morris-Jumel Mansion, Inc., a nonprofit organization, administers the museum. Only 1.5 of the original 130 acres of the old Morris estate remain. The rest of the land has been parceled out, divided into lots of varying sizes over the years. The house sits in the middle of a small park, adjacent to fine **row houses** and surrounded by tall apartment buildings. The view in all directions is of contemporary New York City.

City Hall

30

City Hall

1803–1812

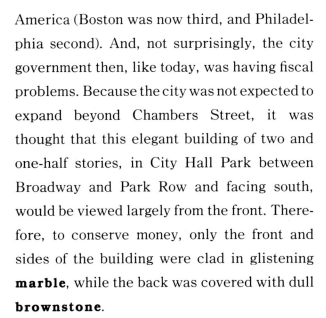

From 1765, when the Morris-Jumel Mansion was built, to the early years of the nineteenth century, when City Hall was designed and built, the population of New York City increased from twenty thousand to one hundred thousand. New York had zoomed past Boston and was by far the largest city in North

America (Boston was now third, and Philadelphia second). And, not surprisingly, the city government then, like today, was having fiscal problems. Because the city was not expected to expand beyond Chambers Street, it was thought that this elegant building of two and one-half stories, in City Hall Park between Broadway and Park Row and facing south, would be viewed largely from the front. Therefore, to conserve money, only the front and sides of the building were clad in glistening **marble**, while the back was covered with dull **brownstone**.

Today, New York has more than seven million residents and City Hall is close to the very southernmost part of Manhattan. More than seventy city agencies employ almost a quarter-million people—more than twice the population of New York City when City Hall was completed!—including approximately 35,000 in the Police Department, 13,000 in the Fire Department, 10,000 in the Sanitation Department, and 2,600 in the Parks and Recreation Department. And, in 1992, all of this activity still flows out of one City Hall, the same City Hall that ran New York one hundred and eighty years ago, in 1812, when DeWitt Clinton was mayor of New York and James Madison was president of the United States.

The current City Hall is New York's third. The first City Hall was originally a tavern (since demolished) and was situated on Pearl Street at Coenties Slip, facing the East River. It became City Hall when New Amsterdam was declared a municipality in 1653.

The second, built at the beginning of the eighteenth century, was situated on Wall and Broad streets. Much of the material for this building came from the wall that the Dutch had built for protection from the English, extending from the East River. Wall Street, just seven blocks long and home to the New York Stock Exchange, was named for that early wall. In 1776, American patriots proclaimed the Declaration of Independence from the steps of this City Hall. The building was renamed Federal Hall in 1789, when it served for a season as the United States Capitol. In the 1790s, it began to deteriorate. When it was demolished in 1812, the scrap was sold for $425.

In February of 1802, the Corporation of the City of New York, aware that New York had no notable public buildings comparable to those in Philadelphia and Boston, offered a $350 prize for the design and **plan** of a new courthouse and City Hall. An advertisement from the *American Citizen and General Advertiser,* dated February 20, 1802, describes the requirements of the building: "The interior arrangement of the building must comprise four courtrooms, two large and two small, six rooms for jurors, eight for public offices, one for the Common Council, and appropriate rooms for the City Watch [as the police were then called], and the housekeeper in the vestibule or wings."

A portion of the large site—now known as City Hall Park—had been occupied by three buildings for the city's less fortunate. The oldest was the Almshouse, a home for the poor, completed in 1734 and ordered to be demol-

ished in 1797. In 1989, excavation for repairs behind City Hall unearthed what many believed to be the remains of the Almshouse. Work was delayed while archaeologists dug a trench, finding such **artifacts** of eighteenth-century life as **pewter** and bone buttons, darning needles, pieces of broken pottery, and oyster shells (oysters have always been popular on many New York menus).

Still standing long after City Hall was completed were two prisons. The Bridewell had been built in 1774 as a jail for vagrants—as the homeless were then called—who roamed New York's streets. Also used as a British prison for American soldiers captured during the Revolution, it was demolished in 1838. The Gaol, or Provost Jail, was later converted into the old Hall of Records. It was torn down in 1903.

In October 1802, eight months after the City Hall **design competition** had been announced, the plans of Joseph-François Mangin, a France-speaking emigré to the United

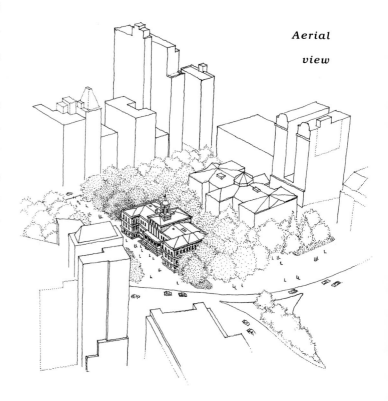

Aerial view

States, and John McComb, Jr., America's first native-born architect, were chosen from the twenty-six that had been received. McComb was appointed architect at a fee of six dollars per day, and the city put aside twenty-five thousand dollars for construction of the building. On March 22, 1803, McComb was appointed sole supervising architect of the building's construction. There is controversy over the exact roles that each architect played, but McComb greatly revised the form of the building and the name of Mangin was not included on the cornerstone, which was laid on May 26, 1803. McComb made substantial changes to the **cupola** and the **rotunda**, and designed all the interior chambers.

The award-winning design proved far costlier than the city had anticipated, however, and the plans had to be scaled down. This is when it was decided to use marble (from Stockbridge, Massachusetts) only for the front and sides of the building, with brownstone (from Newark, New Jersey) for the back. Most of the sculptural ornamentation in the architects' **renderings** was eliminated, the **domed** cupola was simplified, and the wings of the building were made smaller. The nine-year construction project, which began in 1803, cost about three hundred thousand dollars, approximately twelve times the original estimate.

Though the Common Council—as the City Council was then called—and the mayor moved into offices in the building in April, 1812, and a dedication ceremony was held on May 5 of that year, construction was not actually completed until the following year. Soon, travelers' guides were advertising City Hall as a tourist attraction. *Blunt's Stranger's Guide to the City of New York* (1817) enthusiastically described it as "the most prominent, and most important, building in New York. It is the handsomest structure in the United States; perhaps of its size, in the world. . . ."

Originally, City Hall housed a wide variety of functions. In addition to the mayor's office, there was a wine and beer cellar, a kitchen, offices for the police, the city clerk, the clerk of the Supreme Court, and a jail for the Criminal Court in the basement of the building. The kitchen served the tearoom on the first floor, where council members could eat and drink. A receipt from the month of December, 1852, itemizes the following: "beef, pork, vegetables, bread, butter, tea, coffee, milk, sugar, chickens, oysters, eggs, cake, pepper, mustard, salt, vinegar, and help," with a total cost of $776.46. The tearoom was closed in 1853 due to scandals involving the expense of its operation.

The mayor's office was situated in the east wing of the building, and City Court officials occupied the west wing. The third floor of City Hall was originally only a half-story attic space, but after a fire in 1858, the space was rebuilt as a full story, providing an apartment for the building's janitor and his family. When the city's Art Commission was housed on the third floor in 1914, the janitor was evicted.

The U-shaped building has two wings jutting out **symmetrically** on either side of a central structure that is dominated by the front entrance, which is shielded by a one-story **Ionic portico** atop a flight of broad marble steps. Viewed in its entirety, City Hall has a proportion and simplicity characteristic of the **Federal Style**, known for its clean lines and rectangular forms. And the building's ornamentation shows the influence of its French design partner, Mangin. In fact, the great

Clock tower

windows on City Hall's main floor have inspired comparisons to *orangeries,* or French palace greenhouses. The large **arched** windows are evenly spaced between **Corinthian pilasters**. The square-headed windows on the top floor are festooned with swags, or design flourishes, cast in stone. The roof and the portico over the entrance are flat decks encircled by low **balustrades**. (Do you remember that when the Jumels made Federal Style renovations to their **mansion**, they also added balustrades to the roof?)

The building is topped by an elegant, though diminutive, clock tower with a cupola crowned by a copper figure of Justice.

Today, the mayor's offices are on the first floor of the west wing, with the City Council president's office directly opposite in the east wing. This floor also houses the Blue Room, used for the mayor's public meetings, as well as the deputy mayors' offices, the pressroom, and a large executive office, across from the City Council president's office, that is used by the fifty-one members of the City Council.

Upon entering City Hall, the first view is of a magnificent double staircase that sweepingly defines the central rotunda under a small dome. The rotunda (a large, round room) is based on a design concept dating back to the Pantheon (A.D. 118–125), a great round building in Rome originally built as a temple to all the gods. Many important public buildings in the United States—the United States Capitol and the law library at the University of Virginia (designed by Thomas Jefferson) are two examples—are built around central rotundas. City Hall's stairway begins in the center of the room and divides into two flights at the first landing, each of which gracefully sweeps upward in opposite directions to join again on the second floor, just in front of the entrance to the Governor's Room. It is here that Abraham Lincoln's body lay in state after the sixteenth president was assassinated in April, 1865.

The stairway, which seems to be suspended in air, was built using **keystone** construction, an architectural technique most commonly used in arches. In this case, the top step acts as a keystone to lock all the other steps into place. The dome above the staircase is supported by ten Corinthian **columns**.

The west wing of City Hall's second floor

houses the chambers of the City Council, a splendid mahogany-paneled room with a gallery for spectators who overflow from the floor of the chamber. Since January, 1992, the City Council comprises fifty-one representatives from districts throughout the city and is vested with the power to adopt local laws. The City Council was originally the Board of Aldermen, established in 1665. In 1830, the Common Council was set up to include the Board of Aldermen and the Board of Assistant Aldermen, and it was renamed the City Council in 1938.

Directly opposite the City Council chambers, in the east wing, is the room used by the governing body that was called the Board of Estimate until it was disbanded by the Charter Reform referendum approved by New York City voters in 1990. The room, now called the Public Hearing Room, bears a resemblance to the interior of a New England church, with austere white walls and benches arranged like pews, befitting the clean Federal Style that characterizes much of the building's interior.

The Governor's Room, originally in the middle of three rooms that have since been consolidated, in the center front of the second story, was established as the New York City headquarters for the governor when he visited from the state capitol in Albany, although it has not

Rotunda

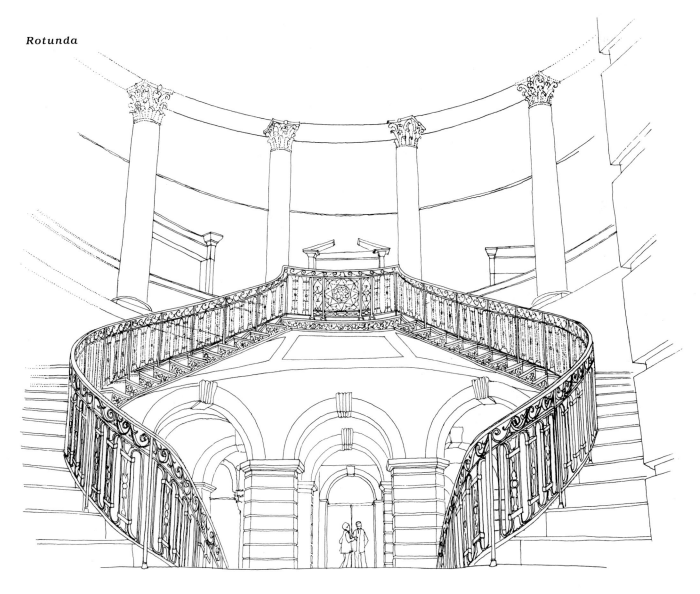

been used for that purpose since the early nineteenth century. For most of City Hall's history, the light, expansive suite has been used on ceremonial occasions and as a **portrait** gallery for some of the city's extensive collection of paintings (which are part of the stewardship of the New York City Art Commission).

This showcase of City Hall was furnished with an appropriation of one thousand dollars from the state legislature in 1814. This money purchased twenty-four richly carved chairs with stuffed backs and seats, two matching sofas, two dining tables, and two "antique" writing tables (antique refers here to style rather than age—they were made by Charles Christian in 1814). A "young Bostonian" writing for the New York *Weekly Museum* said: "The Governor's room is a superb apartment. Rich Turkey carpets, mahogany chairs and tables, with splendid crimson and silk curtains, together with nine half portraits of our great civilians and politicians, and an equal number of full-length likenesses of our naval and military heroes, all richly painted, in elegant frames, fill the mind with a pageant of rich ideas." Since then, the room has been refurbished several times, most recently in 1983 by noted interior and hotel designer Sarah Tomerlin Lee. In the Governor's Room today, you can find a desk used by George Washington when New York City was the nation's capital. It was transferred to City Hall in 1844, along with two high-backed sofas used by the first Congress of the United States at Federal Hall.

City Hall's renowned art collection contains some of the most important portraits in New York City, the earliest dating to 1620. Paintings include John Trumbull's portraits of George Washington; of Alexander Hamilton, the first United States secretary of the treasury; and of John Jay, author of the New York State Constitution and first chief justice of the United States; there are also portraits of several other presidents, statesmen, and war heroes. The paintings are hung throughout the building and are moved from time to time. After Mayor John Lindsay jokingly complained that James Monroe's legs "stole the show" every time the mayor gave a televised press conference beneath the portrait of the fifth president in the Blue Room, it was replaced by one of Martin Van Buren, the country's eighth president, which was less distracting.

In addition to its portraits, the collection has several sculptures, including a **bust** of DeWitt Clinton by the sculptor Enrico Causici. Though Clinton served in the United States House and Senate, as mayor of New York City, and as governor of New York State, what he is best known for is the Erie Canal, which opened in 1825. It was his idea to build a canal from the Hudson River to Lake Erie, linking New York City to Chicago by water, and he oversaw the construction of what was for a time known as "Clinton's Ditch."

City Hall has undergone various renovations—due to wear and tear as well as fires—over the years. It was nearly relocated on more than one occasion. In 1854, the Board of Aldermen considered a plan to move City Hall to Madison Square Park, at Fifth Avenue and 23rd Street. Another option that was considered was to move it to a building that took twenty years to construct (1861–81) at the north end of City Hall Park. This building, a designated landmark formerly called the New York County Courthouse and now known simply as 52 Chambers Street, currently contains city offices that City Hall cannot accommodate. It was originally named after William Marcy ("Boss") Tweed, who was infamous for using his position to reward his circle of cronies within city government, and who exercised tight control over the Democratic party. Tweed is said to have misappropriated more than $30 million of city funds, and his downfall, during the construction of the Tweed Building, is one reason that City Hall never moved from its current location to the building that bore his name. New Yorkers, incidentally, continue to refer to the building as the Tweed Courthouse, although the court moved out in 1961.

In 1858, fireworks set off to celebrate the laying of the first transatlantic cable went awry, burning the cupola and much of the third floor of City Hall and badly damaging the Governor's Room. The renovation included expanding the third floor and replacing the clock tower. The cupola was again destroyed by fire in 1917, and then restored by architect Grosvenor Atterbury, who had **renovated** the Governor's Room ten years earlier.

In 1954, the exterior marble, which had been badly eroded, was replaced with Alabama **limestone**, except for the basement level, which was replaced with Missouri red **granite**. The magnificent central staircase was re-treaded with marble (the hand-carved designs along the sides of the stairs were not replaced).

City Hall Park creates an oasis from the density and confusion of lower Manhattan, and is nearly as significant as the building itself. Its nine acres were designated a city park in 1871, but the land was used by the public long before that. It has been a sports field, a place for public executions, a parade ground, and a meeting place. It was here, in 1766, that the Sons of Liberty erected liberty poles to celebrate the repeal of the Stamp Act of 1765; in 1921, the New-York Historical Society erected a replica flagpole on the spot of one of the originals. Another building that once graced City Hall Park is the Vanderlyn Rotunda, built in 1817 by the painter John Vanderlyn as an art center, where paintings could be exhibited. Later, the building was used as a court (1830) and then a post office (1835). It was torn down in 1870. A **mural** of the palace and gardens at Versailles was removed from the building and is now installed in the Vanderlyn Panorama Gallery of the American Wing at the Metropolitan Museum of Art.

In 1867, the lower part of City Hall Park was transferred to the United States Government for a post office. A four-story building, described as "not only the largest post office building in the world, but (with) unequaled facilities and accommodations for the transaction of business," was completed in 1878. Later, when the building welcomed other functions—a law library and a Western Union telegraph office—the city argued that the federal government had forfeited its right to the lease by changing the use stipulated, and regained the title. The post office was torn down in 1939, and the park restored to its natural state.

The park contains two statues: Nathan Hale, a Revolutionary War hero who was hanged by the British in 1776 for spying, is on the west side of the park, and Horace Greeley, founder of the New York *Tribune,* is on the east side. At one time, a marble sculpture called *Civic Virtue* stood in front of City Hall. This massive work, featuring a scantily clad youth, was thought too risqué for its setting, so it was moved in 1940 to Queens Borough Hall, where it can still be seen.

Theodore Roosevelt Birthplace National Historic Site

1848

Throughout the nineteenth century, many middle-class New Yorkers grew up not in farmhouses or in **mansions**, and not in **tenements** either, but in what New Yorkers call **brownstones**. One, whose house was typical of many others, even if his life was exceptional, was Theodore Roosevelt, the only native of New York City to achieve the highest office in the United States, the presidency. He was born in Manhattan on October 27, 1858, and spent the first fourteen years of his life in the comfort of a happy, prosperous family, growing up in a classic, New York **row house** at 28 East 20th Street between Madison Avenue and Park Avenue South, in what was then the most fashionable district of the city. Neither he nor his family could have imagined that the remarkable events of his life would inspire the designation of his birthplace as a national landmark in 1919, the year that he died.

Theodore Roosevelt, or "Teddy," as he was affectionately called by many, was the second of four children born to Theodore Roosevelt,

Sr., a prosperous New York merchant and financier (partner in the family importing firm), and Martha Bulloch, a Southerner from Roswell, Georgia. The first ancestor of the Roosevelt family (the name Roosevelt means "field of roses" in Dutch) to settle in New York was Claus Martenzen van Rosenvelt, who arrived in the port of New Amsterdam from Holland in the 1640s. By the time Theodore and his siblings were born, the descendants of Claus van Rosenvelt had adopted the name Roosevelt, a variation on the original family name, and become well established in the world of trade and commerce (especially as importers of plate glass), as well as socially prominent members of New York society.

Theodore's grandfather Cornelius Roosevelt had purchased two houses built next to, and connected to, each other on East 20th Street, as wedding gifts for two of his sons, Theodore and Robert. "Teddy," grew up in number 28, with his elder sister, Anna; younger sister, Corinne; and younger brother El-

*Theodore
Roosevelt
Birthplace*

39

Parlor

liott. His uncle Robert's family occupied number 26 next door.

The building lot for each house was a rectangular plot of land. In 1811, the city commissioners laid out the city's new streets based on a **gridiron** pattern of avenues—which would run parallel to each other from north to south—and streets—which would run parallel to each other from east to west. This Commissioners' Plan, as it was called, formed a network of rectangular blocks, and virtually all new building lots in Manhattan were rectangular in order to fit in these blocks. Building lots in the nearby borough of Brooklyn tended to be laid out the same way.

New York row houses like the Roosevelts' were generally built on lots that were twenty to twenty-five feet wide by ninety to one hundred feet deep; that is, the houses were narrow from the front, but compensated for their narrow width by the length of the rooms extending toward the back. Because of the high cost of land so close to the center of the city, a row house was always one of a series of houses, connected to one another by common **party walls**, and forming a continuous group. Therefore, with the exception of houses at the corners of blocks, the typical row house could have windows only in the front and back walls—the street side and the garden side. Most row houses were three to four stories high, and three **bays** wide. The street level floor was called the basement, while a flight of stairs, called a **stoop**, led up to the front door on the first, or main, floor. The shallow front yard was enclosed by an iron fence and the small backyard was fenced off from neighboring lots. At the back of the house there was often a **porch**, overlooking a planted garden. Brownstones were built to the size of the lot, and in accordance with an instructional manual for builders, and had standardized arrangements of rooms.

The main room was known as the **parlor**, a sitting room that was located on the first floor at the front of the house. It was the most accessible room to visitors, and was used for entertaining guests. The interiors and fireplaces were often elaborate. The **mantels** were made of carved **marble**, and the ceilings and walls often had richly modeled plaster **molding** as a decorative element. Between the parlor—sometimes it was a double parlor, with the second room used as a study or library—and the dining room at the rear of the building were hidden sliding doors or hinged doors that could be opened and closed depending on the occasion.

The kitchen (meals were usually sent upstairs to the dining room in a **dumbwaiter**), family room, and wood- or coal-storage rooms were located downstairs in the basement, while the upper floors were reserved for the family bedrooms, dressing rooms, sitting rooms, and closets. On the top floor there were small bedrooms for the live-in servants, which sometimes doubled as sewing rooms.

The brownstone that Theodore Roosevelt grew up in was built in 1848, in the **Gothic Revival Style**, by an architect who remains unknown. If you look around a neighborhood of New York City that has many row houses, you will see a great deal of the smooth, reddish brown stone that is called brownstone. This stone, actually a dark red sandstone quarried mostly in Connecticut and New Jersey, had been a cheaper alternative to marble or **granite** for decorative elements of brick buildings in New York City since the early nineteenth century. With the rise of Gothic Revival Style architecture in the mid-1840s, it became fashionable to design full brownstone fronts for row houses. So widespread was the use of brownstone in New York City from the Civil War to the 1890s, when white **limestone** became popular for row houses, that one historian has called those years "the brown decades." By the way, brownstones are actually brick buildings with a thin veneer of brownstone on the front.

Gothic Revival Style row houses like the Roosevelts', which were occasionally built in New York City in the decade and a half before the Civil War, used **Gothic motifs**, usually sparingly, as simple embellishments on an otherwise ordinary building. Gothic elements in the Roosevelt house include the square-headed door hood and window **lintels**, with their **drip moldings**—short, horizontal protrusions—at each end that have the practical function of directing rainwater off the window and door surfaces, as well as the **cornice** decorated by **arches**.

The Roosevelt house had some amenities that were not typical of New York City row houses, such as the full-length windows—actually **French doors**—of the parlor that open onto a **cast-iron balcony**, which allowed the occupants to step out and take in the fresh air without having to leave the house. The shutters were meant to protect the windows from strong winds, but also served to give the **facade** a less severe, warmer look.

An attic with a slate-shingled **mansard** roof was added in 1865. The mansard roof, a sloping roof one or more stories tall, became popular in New York City in the 1850s. Aside from being attractive additions, mansards were an economical way to add extra floors, which received light through **dormer** windows. You can see all kinds of mansard roofs—the style is named after the French architect François Mansart, who invented it—on New York landmarks, including, in this book, The Dakota (see pages 86–91) and the U.S. Custom House (see pages 108–13). There are really splendid convex mansard roofs on the Ansonia Hotel at Broadway and 73rd Street.

The interiors of the Roosevelt house were handsomely decorated by one of the leading cabinetmakers and decorators of the time, Leon Marcotte, in 1865. In his memoirs, Theodore recalled the parlor as the most splendid room. It was used only on Sunday evenings or on special occasions for parties. Behind the parlor was the library, and at the back was the dining room, with horsehair-covered chairs that often scratched the bare legs of the children who sat on them. Theodore's parents occupied the front bedroom on the second floor; it was furnished in a formal style with bed, chairs, dressers, and wardrobes made of rosewood and satinwood veneer. The house was among the first in New York to have indoor plumbing and had the convenience of a bathroom adjacent to the bedrooms.

All four of the Roosevelt children were sickly, especially Theodore, or "Teedie," as he was called by the members of his immediate family. Although he suffered from a severe asthmatic condition, Theodore's perseverance enabled him to overcome the ailment and live normally. Aside from exercising in a special gymnasium that his father had built for him behind the nursery, he indulged his insatiable curiosity by reading books on natural history, as well as fiction and adventure stories, developing a keen literary mind in the process.

In the fall of 1872, the Roosevelt family moved to a new house at 6 West 57th Street (since demolished), renting their earlier home to various small businesses. Once a peaceful residential area, the old 20th Street neighborhood had by then become a busy commercial district. Lord & Taylor, an early department store, opened only a block away at 901 Broadway in 1869, and large commercial establishments such as Tiffany & Co., which moved uptown to a building at Union Square and 15th Street (since demolished), were beginning to dominate the neighborhood. In 1916, the original Roosevelt house was demolished to make room for a two-story commercial building.

Theodore, meanwhile, was graduated from Harvard University in 1880 and married Alice Hathaway Lee, the daughter of a prominent banker, in the same year. His political career began when he was elected to the New York State Assembly in 1881 (he was reelected in 1882 and 1883). The Roosevelts had a daughter, Alice, born on February 12, 1884, whom they named after her mother. Sadly, only two days after her birth, on February 14, her mother died of Bright's disease, an inflammation of the kidneys. Coincidentally, Theodore's mother died on the same day, in the same house on 57th Street. Theodore was reportedly so grieved by his wife's death that he could not call his daughter by her first name, and instead nicknamed her "Baby Lee."

"Baby Lee" grew up and married Congressman Nicholas Longworth of Ohio, but always remained close to her father. Alice Lee Roosevelt Longworth became an outspoken and well-known public figure in her own right, recognized for her candor and wit. She was considered so headstrong in character that her father was known to joke, "I can either be the president of the United States, or I can control Alice." Until her death at the age of ninety-six, on February 20, 1980, she was prominent as a Washington hostess, commentator on public and social events, and philanthropist but always avoided affiliation with institutions. She was often referred to as "Washington's Other Monument," and dozens of songs were written about her, the most famous being "Alice Blue Gown," which led to the naming of the color Alice blue, a slightly grayish shade of blue.

In June, 1884, Theodore, then a widower, moved west to the Dakota Territory, where he worked as a cattle rancher. He returned to New York in 1886 and ran for mayor, but was defeated. After the election, he went to London to marry Edith Kermit Carow (who eventually had five of his children), a childhood friend who had grown up near 14th Street. They had met again soon after his first wife's death, and the romance of their teenage years, interrupted by his departure for school at Harvard, was rekindled.

From 1889 to 1895, Roosevelt served as a commissioner for the Civil Service, and then from 1895 to 1897 as president of the New York Board of Police Commissioners, where he weeded out corruption within the Police Department. In 1897, he was appointed by President William McKinley to serve as the assistant secretary of the United States Navy. However, Roosevelt stunned his peers by resigning from office in May, 1898, to help organize the famous Rough Riders, a volunteer cavalry troop composed of ranchers and cowboys. By the end of June he had his regiment on Cuban soil to fight in the Spanish-American War, in which the Americans were victorious. He won acclaim for leading a charge up San Juan Hill in July.

Roosevelt came home to find himself one of the most celebrated men in America. Even while he was assistant secretary of the navy, his popularity had been growing so fast that Republican politicians were plotting his nomination for governor of New York. He was elected, and served from 1899 to 1901. As governor, he sponsored laws limiting the number of hours that women and children could work and regulating working conditions in **sweatshops**. In 1900, he was persuaded to run for the vice presidency with President William McKinley on the Republican ticket. Their campaign was successful, but on September 6, 1901, President McKinley was mortally wounded by an assassin, and eight days later Theodore Roosevelt assumed the presidency, at forty-two, the youngest president before or since.

Roosevelt's two terms as president (1901–9) were characterized by his ability to be both conservative and progressive at different times, depending on the situation. Of his many accomplishments, he was proudest of his conservation program, which added about 230 million acres, including five national parks, to the national forests. In 1906, he won the Nobel Peace Prize for his participation in mediating the Russo-Japanese War during the years 1904–5. He used the $36,735 prize money to create a trust fund to aid victims of World War I.

In 1908, he endorsed William H. Taft, a Republican, as his successor, rather than run for president again. As he grew dissatisfied with Taft's performance, he decided to oppose him in 1912, by establishing, in an extraordinary act, the Progressive, or "Bull Moose," party, which opposed both the Republican and Democratic parties. The Progressive party lasted from 1912 to 1916, despite Roosevelt's defeat in the 1912 presidential election. Under Roosevelt's leadership the party pressed for many innovative ideas, such as votes for women and pensions for senior citizens, that were adopted in later years.

One of Roosevelt's favorite pastimes was going into the wilderness with friends to hunt wild animals. On one of his many hunting expeditions, in November, 1902, the president was invited by his guide to shoot a bear that the guide had tracked down and roped to a tree. Although his companions urged the president to shoot the bear to keep as a hunting trophy, he felt that it would be unsportsmanlike to do so. The story quickly reached the newspapers, and a famous cartoonist named Clifford Berryman drew a caricature, or cartoon, of the president refusing to shoot a bear being led by a rope.

The cartoon inspired Ideal Toys of Brooklyn, as well as Steiff toymakers in Germany, to make toy stuffed bears, which they called, by permission of the president, "Teddy bears." Did you, or do you, have a Teddy bear? Now you know why this stuffed animal was always treated with affection, and how it got its name. It's hard to believe that Teddy bears have been made only since 1903, because they are such a classic and timeless toy that remains a favor-

ite in many nations. If you visit the Theodore Roosevelt Birthplace, you can see one of these early Teddy bears in its collection of **memorabilia**.

But the Teddy bear is only one of many reminders of Theodore Roosevelt's legacy. Although the original house of his childhood was torn down in 1916, a replica was built in its original location, to symbolize the special sentiment people had for the memory of the twenty-sixth president, his achievements, and the man himself.

Shortly after Theodore Roosevelt's death in 1919 (his health had been declining since he received a leg injury while traveling in Brazil), the site on East 20th Street was purchased by a group of prominent New Yorkers. They had the commercial building demolished and commissioned Theodate Pope Riddle, a leading woman architect of the time, to reconstruct the original house, as it was in 1865 when the attic was added, as a monument to the late president. The site next door, where the other Roosevelt house once stood, was purchased as well and reconstructed as an extension to the Theodore Roosevelt Birthplace.

Theodate Pope Riddle was born in Cleveland, Ohio, and raised as the only child of **steel** magnate Alfred Pope and his wife, Ada Pope. At that time, it was almost unthinkable that a proper young lady should have a career. But Theodate (who changed her given name from Effie to her grandmother's name) grew up shy and lonely, with a need to fulfill her early passion for architecture rather than become a "respectable" society hostess like her mother. In rebellion against her parents' hopes of molding her into a debutante, she requested as a graduation gift a tour through Europe.

There, she saw firsthand the architectural wonders that had fascinated her all her life. Upon her return, she set out to achieve her ambition to become an architect, first restoring an eighteenth-century cottage in Farmington, Connecticut, that her parents had given her as a gift. She arranged to study privately with members of the art department at Princeton University, which was then an institution exclusively attended by men. After graduation, she designed a house for her parents, who hired Stanford White, one of the founding partners of the internationally known architectural firm of McKim, Mead & White, to supervise the construction.

The close association with one of the most prestigious firms in the country gave her the further opportunity to overcome the obstacle of being a woman in a profession that was almost entirely dominated by men. Although she married John Riddle, a United States diplomat to Russia, in 1916, she maintained an office with a practice specializing in residential design. In 1919, her reputation for restoration and residential design caught the attention of the Woman's Roosevelt Memorial Association, formed in the same year to honor the memory of the late president.

The restoration project was a difficult one, as there were very few photographs and house **plans** to use as guidelines. The main sources of help came from the surviving members of the Roosevelt family—Theodore's two sisters, who had both grown up in the house—as well as from his widow. The cost of rebuilding the house came to $500,000, which included building an office and library on the top floors in conjunction with the museum. The money was raised by the Woman's Roosevelt Memorial Association, a New York organization, and the Roosevelt Memorial Association, a national organization, which eventually merged to become the present Theodore Roosevelt Association. To refurnish the house, the architect and the Woman's Roosevelt Memorial Association recovered nearly 40 percent of the original furnishings, with the remainder coming from other family collections or period pieces.

On October 27, 1923, the sixty-fifth anniversary of Teddy's birth, the museum/memorial was opened to the public. Since that time the house has been a museum and has been used for concerts, lectures, student contests, and award ceremonies. In 1963, the Theodore Roosevelt Association donated the site to the National Park Service. In 1977, the National Park Service extensively restored the house. Paint samples, wall coverings, fabric swatches, and carpet samples in every part of the house were researched, and colors and patterns were painstakingly reproduced, so that you, too, can experience the nineteenth-century interiors with which Theodore Roosevelt grew up.

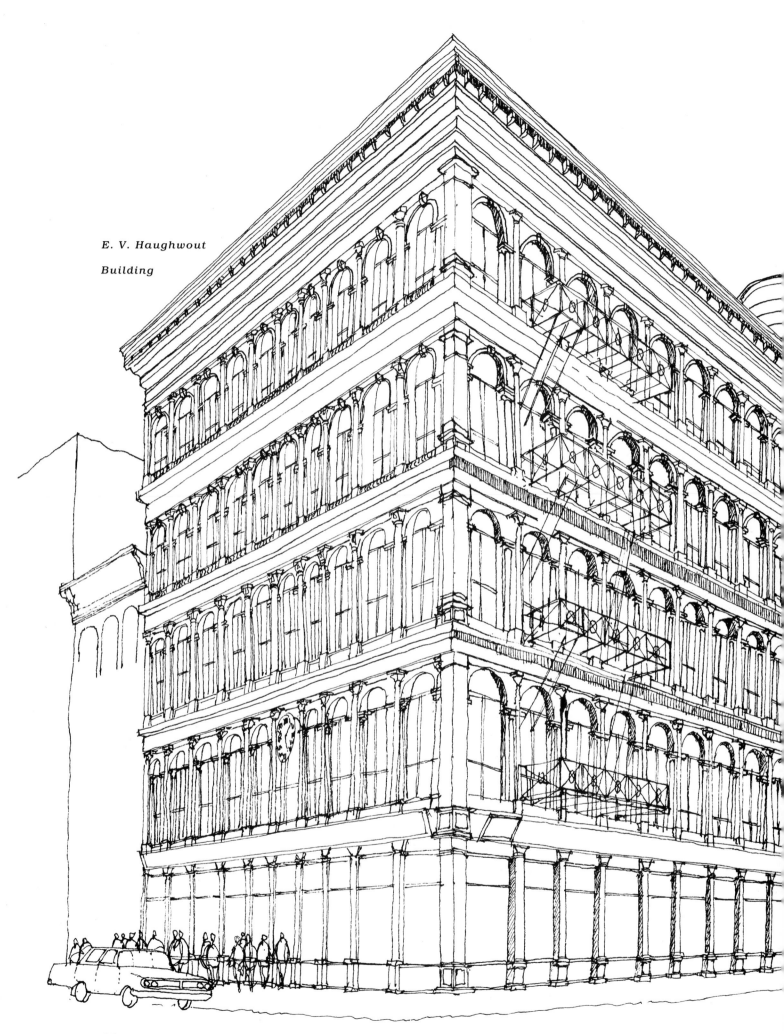

E. V. Haughwout
Building

46

E. V. Haughwout Building

1856

In the twenty years between 1840 and 1860, the population of the area within the current boundaries of New York City—Manhattan, Brooklyn, Queens, the Bronx, and Staten Island—grew faster than it has either before or since. When the Civil War began in 1861, there were over one million people living in this area, and over eight hundred thousand in Manhattan alone. It is to this period, when intense population growth and frenetic economic development placed heavy demands on the available space in lower Manhattan, that we can trace the origins of New York as a city of tall buildings.

Nowadays, the skyline of New York City is studded with **skyscrapers**, which are its most dazzling architectural feature. They are the reason New York seems to dwarf other cities. A long history of technological in-novation paved the way for the modern sky-scraper. The most important precursor of the skyscraper was the **cast-iron building**, whose invention reflected the commercial and industrial power that surged through New York between the years 1840 and 1860. In both its materials and construction, the cast-iron building was made possible by the processes of mass production and standardization that be-gan to transform America during these years.

Although many of these predecessors of the modern skyscraper were destroyed or disman-tled over the years, over two hundred and fifty cast-iron buildings survive in Manhattan, with a concentration of them in the area known as "SoHo" (short for "South of Houston Street"). One of the earliest and best examples of cast-iron architecture is the 1856 E. V. Haughwout Building, at 488 Broadway on the corner of Broome Street.

SoHo, just south of Greenwich Village and now one of the most popular strolling and shop-ping areas in New York City, is a neighborhood of artists' studios, art galleries, trendy fashion and home furnishings boutiques, cafés, and popular restaurants, as well as some large dis-count warehouses. From 1900 until 1960, the area had been forgotten and sorely neglected.

By the mid-1960s artists began moving their studios into cavernous loft spaces that had been deserted for many years. The low rents, generous work space, and good light allowed them the opportunity to work with greater ease and stability. As a result of their initiative, followed by an important change in the city **zoning** laws that legally permitted the conversion of commercial space to residential use and offered incentives to do so, SoHo was revitalized into one of the leading centers for contemporary art in the world.

Use your imagination to envision a past in which this bustling urban area was farmland. Here was the first settlement granted to freed black slaves in New York. During the mid-seventeenth century, when the land was still predominantly in the hands of the Dutch, farms were given to black slaves who had been freed after serving the Dutch West India Company for twenty years. They were permitted to make their own living as farmers, although they did not enjoy all the same privileges and treatment as their white counterparts.

During the 1770s, at the time of the Revolution, numerous forts were constructed north of the city, with at least four located in what is now SoHo. The financial pressures of the Revolutionary War forced landowners to divide their **estates** into lots, and by the 1790s, some small manufacturing businesses had already moved in, prompting the development of the land and the paving of the streets.

Middle-class families began moving into the area as well, spurring the construction of **Federal Style row houses**, a few of which survive. Several prominent members of the New York community, such as the Reverend John Livingston; Citizen Genet, the French diplomat who was sent as minister to the United States during the French Revolution; and James Fenimore Cooper, the first major American novelist, who wrote about the American frontier, took up residence, giving the neighborhood an air of prestige. By the 1820s, SoHo—of course, it wasn't called that then—was the most populous section of New York.

Until about 1850, the area maintained its status as a respectable residential neighborhood, with cobbled streets and blocks of family row houses. In the 1850s, larger commercial businesses began to replace the small, brick retail shops on Broadway with immense structures of gleaming cast iron and **marble**. Along with department stores such as Lord & Taylor (at Broadway and Grand Street from 1860 to 1872), Tiffany & Co. (at 550 Broadway from 1854 to 1870, since demolished), and E. V. Haughwout (1856–69), major hotels, music halls, and theaters began to line Broadway. The intensity of commerce and entertainment in the neighborhood made it less desirable for families to live there.

It was during this time that commercial architecture began to develop rapidly. As a result of the Industrial Revolution, iron was becoming a key building material; it was stronger than such traditional materials as wood and brick, as well as more versatile and seemingly fireproof.

Iron is a silvery gray, soft metal that is found in a variety of metal-enriched minerals, or ores, in the earth's crust, such as hematite, pyrite, and magnetite, as well as in meteorites, which contain about 80 to 95 percent iron. These ores are extracted from the ground by mining. A blast furnace, a special "oven" that reaches very high temperatures, is required to separate

Detail of the facade and cornice

By the mid-nineteenth century, on the other hand, cast iron could be produced in a faster and more economical way. The impurities in the pig iron are removed not by hammering but by a melting process, and then the iron is cast, or poured into a mold while still in molten form, to give it shape.

Steel is a commercial form of iron that is harder and stronger than cast iron. The techniques required to produce steel on a broad scale became available only in the 1850s, and it was many years before steel was routinely used in building construction. It was first used in heavy construction in America for John Roebling's Brooklyn Bridge (see pages 62–73).

Before the late eighteenth century, iron was used in Europe for tools, cooking utensils, firearms, and decorative architectural elements, such as fences and gates. It was not until the 1770s, when English engineers and architects began using it for bridges, that cast iron was accepted as a primary building material. In 1792, an Englishman named Jedediah Strutt, who had textile mills in the towns of Derby and Belper, used vertical pieces of ironwork to support timber **beams**. Others followed his lead, and by 1807, at least seven mills in England had iron, instead of wood, frames, and many more were built with interior iron **columns**, instead of interior walls that would obstruct the open spaces required for heavy machinery.

The English developed a method of **prefabrication** of iron building frames soon after they

pig iron, a crude form of iron, from these ores.

The pig iron can be further refined to produce **wrought iron**, cast iron, or **steel**. Wrought iron appeared as early as the fifth century B.C. in Greece, and was put to use in the making of small objects, such as window frames and tie rods. It was called wrought iron because it had to be hammered, or "wrought," while hot, first to remove the impurities remaining from the original ore, and then to fashion it into the desired shape. This was time-consuming and laborious work.

began to use iron for structural support. Prefabrication greatly increased the speed of construction. It involved making standardized parts in great quantities, and in a wide variety of styles, at iron **foundries**, and then assembling the individual buildings on their sites. In this way English foundries made frames and other parts for buildings that were exported all across the world: houses, churches, mills, and warehouses are just a few examples. The foundries even had catalogues available so that customers could order a particular style of building by mail.

Iron rarely replaced wood completely in American architecture, because wood was relatively cheap and abundant. But building fronts made completely from cast iron were first conceived in America by James Bogardus, who was a New York manufacturer (his 1862 cast-iron warehouse at 85 Leonard Street still exists) and inventor rather than an architect or engineer. Born in Catskill, New York, in 1800, he made a trip to Europe in 1836, where he was educated in the Classical forms of architecture. His designs show us that Italian **Renaissance** architecture influenced him greatly, particularly the proportions and ornamentation of the architect Jacopo Sansovino's St. Mark's Library (1536) in Venice. (His other inventions included items that we still use today, such as the gas meter, the metal-encased pencil, and an engraving machine for printing postage stamps.) Although he obtained a patent in 1850 for the mass production of prefabricated buildings, Bogardus's techniques were widely imitated, and he soon had numerous competitors in the manufacture of cast iron building fronts, which were far more common than all-iron buildings.

The superior strength of iron introduced into architecture what was eventually to become the basic principle of skyscraper design. While an iron-front structure was still somewhat reliant on **masonry load-bearing walls** for its support, the street **facade**—or facades, if the building was on a corner—utilized iron walls, which could be much lighter than masonry walls and bear the same amount of weight. The strength of cast iron under compression permitted the use of slender **piers** between large windows, letting maximum sunlight into the interior of the building, which was ideal for retail businesses and factories. (In true skyscraper design, the exterior walls have *no* load-bearing function! See the discussion of Lever House and the Seagram Building on pages 146–50.)

It was also hoped that cast-iron construction would offer protection against the ever-present danger of fire. But although the metal could not burn and would melt only at extreme temperatures, the floors, walls, and ceilings of cast-iron buildings continued to be constructed of wood and plaster, which would burn during a fire. Hot iron might crack when, during an attempt to put out a fire, it was doused with cold water. This, firefighters quickly learned, made it hazardous to control a fire in a cast-iron building. As we know, fire is still a hazard, even in modern, high-tech skyscrapers.

The early cast-iron facades most often chosen were variations on Venetian Renaissance designs, which were considered a welcome stylistic diversion from the austere Federal Style buildings that dominated the architecture of the city before the 1850s. Later, **High Victorian Italianate** and the French **Second Empire Style** became popular. The elements included in these styles were various versions of the **Classical orders**, consisting of columns, each with a **base**, a **shaft**, and a **capital**, with **pediments** and **entablatures**. These constituent parts could be standardized and mass-produced in the medium of iron, as the same piece could be cast as many times as necessary. And while stone and marble, the traditional materials employed in the construction of buildings that utilized the Classical orders, weathered after years of exposure to the elements, eventually losing their clarity of form, cast iron retained its definitive contours and sharpness of detail. The only maintenance required was an occasional paint job, and the majority of cast-iron buildings were painted in hues that resembled stone and marble, to give them the luxurious appearance of masonry **palazzi**. (If you would like to be able to identify iron-front buildings in New York, many of which have been painted to look like stone, you would do well to carry a small magnet!)

The idea of a "palace" of commerce gave the E. V. Haughwout Building its distinguishing features. The site on which it was built was farmland originally belonging to John Jacob Astor, who left eight city lots to his three grandsons when he died in 1848. The eldest, Walter Langdon, owned the lot at Broome Street, which he later either leased or sold to Eder V. Haughwout, a successful merchant in such dry goods as porcelain, china, chandeliers, cut glass, silverware, and clocks. His merchandise was known to be of such fine quality that he became a frequent supplier of china to the White House. The five-story structure, built on a corner lot in 1856, was ideal for a department store, as there was plenty of space available for a fanciful display of merchandise, as well as abundant daytime light that poured in through the enormous windows.

J. P. Gaynor, the architect of the E. V. Haughwout Building, favored the stately, **ornate** Venetian style, with large **arched** windows framed between columns, considered appropriate in the 1850s for commercial buildings. In his design, he struck the perfect balance between the vertical and horizontal elements of the structure. The standardized element in the design, as in many cast-iron buildings, is the basic window unit, in this case a **keystone** arch resting on freestanding **Corinthian colonnettes**, which is repeated a total of ninety-two times on the two facades. The colonnettes carry the eye upward, balancing the horizontal pattern created by the four tiers of windows, each resting on a full entablature, and by the bold **cornice** that crowns the building. The ground floor is distinguished from the four upper floors by its greater height and simpler decoration. The entrance on Broadway is located at the center of the building, further emphasized by a large clock above the doorway. The play of light and shadow on the surface of the facade gives the building a sculptural quality.

The elements were cast by Daniel D. Badger, a blacksmith from New Hampshire. In fact, his fabrication of the facade of the E. V. Haughwout Building made him famous. Badger had opened a foundry in Boston in 1829, which by 1842 had erected a cast-iron store front, which Badger claimed was the earliest in existence, although cast-iron store fronts were advertised in New York City as early as 1829. Moving to New York in 1846, he established a small foundry, called the Architectural Iron Works, at 42 Duane Street (since demolished).

In 1854, he expanded his business and built a huge foundry on 14th Street between Avenue B and Avenue C. Although Badger did not design building parts, his Architectural Iron Works had an architectural department headed by a professional architect.

The heyday of cast-iron building in this area came after the Civil War, but the techniques developed by Bogardus and Badger were not significantly improved upon. By the end of the 1860s, the department stores were moving uptown, north of 14th Street. The E. V. Haughwout store closed in 1869. SoHo then became a center for manufacturing, and the cast-iron building was truly king. Most of the factories and warehouses with cast-iron fronts in SoHo were built between 1860 and 1890, for cast-iron construction—when combined with the use of brick for **party walls** and of wood floors and beams—continued to be efficient and economical even when it was no longer considered stylish for the big, elaborate retail emporiums that have always stood out in New York City.

Today, the E. V. Haughwout Building is owned by the Broadway Mfrs. Supply Corp., which sells such cotton goods as bed linens, towels, and table linens. The company still maintains and uses a nineteenth-century elevator reminiscent of the building's original passenger safety elevator, the world's first. This,

Elevator enclosure on the ground floor

another harbinger of the coming of the skyscraper, was invented in 1852 by Elisha G. Otis and installed in 1857 when the building was new. Although the building has been kept from deteriorating, it is still in great need of repair and restoration. As it is one of the most notable cast-iron buildings in the city, it is hoped that one day it will be restored to its original splendor for the benefit of the public's enjoyment of beautiful and historic architecture.

Central Park

Begun 1857

Central Park, a ribbon of vibrant green adorning Manhattan Island, is a vital part of our city. Conceived in 1856, long before the land around it was developed, it was one of the first architectural projects in America built on a grand scale in accordance with a **master plan**. Designed by two of America's premier landscape architects, Frederick Law Olmsted and Calvert Vaux, when both were still remarkably young, it was the first great urban park in the United States, encouraging a community spirit compatible with the ideals of freedom and democracy of the growing nation. Its naturalistic setting provided a beautiful country retreat in the midst of the city, accessible to all citizens, regardless of wealth or status.

New Yorkers have always been proud of their city as a place of rapid change and explosive growth. In 1811, when City Hall (see pages 30–37) marked the northern edge of development, the city commissioners thought nothing of laying out a **gridiron** pattern of future streets deep into the farmlands of northern Manhattan. The Commissioners' Plan, as it was called, designated the area bounded by 23rd and 34th streets and Third and Seventh avenues as a park. Thirty-six years later in 1847, when Madison Square Park actually opened, the farmland was only a memory, and **real-estate development** had so nibbled away at the park that it covered less than three square city blocks. Even when you included City Hall Park, Bowling Green, Washington Square, Gramercy Park, and Stuyvesant Square, there was not a lot of recreational space for a city of a half-million people. Not one of these parks was big enough even for a baseball game (baseball was invented about 1839).

And the people kept coming and the builders kept building. Immigration was one of the great forces that shaped New York. In the decade of the 1830s, the United States government counted over a half-million immigrants entering this country; in the 1840s, almost two million. By far the most common port of entry was New York City. In 1855, the city converted a huge concert hall called Castle Garden (now a designated landmark called Castle Clinton National Monument, and originally a fort called West Battery) at the Battery into the nation's first Emigrant Landing Depot. A survey in that year determined that the average life savings brought by immigrants was eighty-six dollars and that two out of five planned to remain in New York City. Most of these immigrants were either Irish Catholics entering a predominantly Protestant city, or Germans who spoke no English.

Belvedere Castle

It is no wonder that many citizens began to worry about the future health of their city: not only was it growing too fast, but it was also becoming more crowded and more diverse, and it was clearly developing a sharply divided class system. With growth and **diversity** came a loss of feeling of community, and a threat to the ideals of democracy.

Furthermore, the crowding itself made the city an unhealthy place in which to live. Few houses had toilets (Teddy Roosevelt's father was among the first to install one in his house; see pages 38–45), and in poor areas, sewage from **outhouses** often contaminated the drinking water in wells, causing epidemics of cholera and other diseases. For the first time, the appreciation and preservation of nature in an industrialized society became an issue of public awareness and concern.

How could nature be brought back into city life? What institution could bring together people of different religion, nationality, race, and class as equals? Frederick Law Olmsted thought he knew the answer, and he confirmed it when he strolled through his almost completed Central Park in 1870 and saw "vast numbers of persons brought closely together, poor and rich, young and old, Jew and Gentile."

The earliest calls for a big public park came in the 1840s. Beginning in 1844, William Cullen Bryant, well-known poet, orator, and editor of the New York *Evening Post*, used the paper to campaign for one. Landscape architect Andrew Jackson Downing added his voice in his magazine, the *Horticulturist*. By 1850, it was an issue in the mayoral elections, and the victorious Mayor Ambrose C. Kingsland got the City Council to approve the addition of a park to the city plan a year later. Politicians tended to fa-

vor the project, which would provide jobs for thousands of men who would be needed to clear the land of rocks and weeds, and spread soil over the rocky terrain to reshape whatever site was chosen. In those days before heavy earth-moving equipment existed, it was clear that a large labor force would be needed.

Originally, a site along the East River was proposed. The city, however, saw that property as a potentially profitable one and wanted to develop the waterfront for commerce and business. As a result, a much less impressive site, a long, narrow, and somewhat swampy strip of land between Fifth and Eighth avenues from 59th to 106th street, was chosen. The city obtained the State Legislature's authority to buy the land in 1853. After the park was extended to 110th Street in 1859, the site covered 843 acres. This inspired a major real-estate boom around the park's perimeter, as wealthy New York families rushed to buy this previously undesirable land and build their country manors and **villas** overlooking the park. A board of commissioners was appointed to oversee the construction **plan** of the park, and in October of 1857, a **design competition** was announced.

The design competition brought together two very gifted architects, Frederick Law Olmsted and Calvert Vaux. Olmsted was thirty-five years old and had never, so far as is known, designed anything. He had been a farmer, reporter, publisher, and nurseryman, and was just settling into his job as superintendent of the enormous work crew hired to clear the park site of rocks and trees. Calvert Vaux, thirty-three, an English architect recently moved to America, approached him to suggest they collaborate on a design. Vaux had come to the United States in 1850 to work as an archi-

Bow Bridge

tectural assistant to landscape designer Andrew Jackson Downing. Downing had been commissioned to design some prestigious projects, including the grounds of the United States Capitol and the White House, and almost certainly would have been selected to design New York's new park as well, had he not been killed in 1852 in a steamboat accident on the Hudson River, leaving Vaux to establish his architectural reputation on his own. Olmsted agreed to collaborate with Vaux on the design of the park; he worked by day with the laboring men, and by night with Vaux, envisioning the dramatic transformation of the site. Their plan, which they named "Greensward," won, and on April 1, 1858, it became the official blueprint for Central Park, with Olmsted and Vaux overseeing construction every step of the way.

Olmsted and Vaux had strong ideas about what their park should look like, and what it should represent. They sought to create a respite from the brick and stone of the en-

croaching city, in a naturalistic, picturesque environment, and so they created an unrestricted design with irregular, flowing lines, one in which the works of man seem secondary to the beauty of nature.

In most European countries, the idea of a park meant either a formal garden or the hunting ground of an **estate**. The gardens, laid out geometrically with straight, tree-lined avenues and perfectly circular flower beds, were rather artificial, clearly establishing the role of mankind over nature, while the more naturally landscaped grounds of noblemen's estates were restricted to use by only the wealthiest.

In Central Park, Olmsted and Vaux created a vast noble estate free to all. They believed that the park should avoid the intrusions of civilization wherever possible. There should be no buildings in a park, they decided, unless those buildings served a specific park purpose; any other architecture, like bridges, **arches**, shelters, and even roadways, should blend har-

Rustic shelter

moniously into the landscape. Olmsted accepted the building of Belvedere Castle only because he felt the need for a dramatic **vista** from the Bethesda Terrace and no natural solution presented itself.

Olmsted, as chief architect, was responsible for arranging the **topography** of the park, creating gentle slopes, waterways, wooded areas, and open fields, and he chose the trees and bushes that would be planted. The land he had to work with was not ideal. This strip of Manhattan Island was rocky and uneven, with swamp more common than dry land. Most of the rocks he had cleared away, although some of the boulders and craggy rock outcroppings (enjoyed by rock-climbers of all ages) were appreciated for their dramatic appearance and were highlighted, rather than hidden. Swampy areas were drained and sometimes replaced by clear pools and lakes. To even out the rough terrain, ten million one-horse-cartloads of dirt were towed to the site and raked out over the ground by hand. Plantings included four to five million trees representing 632 species, and 815 varieties of vines, plants, and flowers.

Calvert Vaux, as assistant architect, was responsible for the architectural elements of the park: the bridges, archways, buildings, and

rustic shelters that combined with the landscaping to create the picturesque scenes we still find today in Central Park. Vaux hired an associate, Jacob Wrey Mould, and together they created a wide variety of structures, ranging from the grand Bethesda Terrace to the most unobtrusive footbridge. Their impressive designs, an array ranging from showy to subtle, were both aesthetic and practical.

Even from the street, the park declares its democratic ideals. Olmsted and Vaux refused to construct the imposing, formal gateways that adorn European parks. They envisioned the park as an entirely public place, open and available to all: a reflection of the nation's values. One can enter the park through any one of twenty-two simple, unobtrusive openings in the perimeter wall. Have you ever noticed that these unintimidating entrances are named to represent all types of people in many walks of life? Beginning at Columbus Circle, at the southwest corner of the park, then proceeding clockwise, the gates are Merchants, Women, Naturalists (across from the American Museum of Natural History), Hunters, Mariners, Prophets, Boys, Strangers (that is, foreigners), Warriors, Farmers, Pioneers, Girls, Woodmen, Engineers, Miners, Inventors, Students, Children (appropriately placed at the entrance to the Central Park Zoo), Scholars, Artists, and Artisans. Dedicating the gates in this way underscores the idea of the park as a truly public place, belonging to everyone.

Once inside the park, the visitor needed pathways. Olmsted and Vaux wanted many people to be able to roam easily throughout the park while still feeling somewhat solitary and removed from the crowds of the city. Handling traffic, then, became a primary concern, and the designers did not want to overwhelm the naturalistic setting with too many roads. Their plan called for three kinds of roads, each for a different mode of transportation: carriage roads, bridle paths (for horseback riders), and footpaths. Remember, when the park was built, the horse-drawn carriage was the main means of transportation, and horseback riding was a popular form of recreation as well. The roads Olmsted and Vaux designed were deliberately **sinuous**, to discourage racing and encourage the visitor to go at a slow pace and appreciate the scenery.

In order that these three road systems not create too many intersections, wandering park-goers pass over and under each other on bridges and through archways. The next time you are in the park, why don't you make a special effort to pay attention to them: they are each unique in size, shape, and ornament, perhaps in imitation of the ceaseless variety found in nature, and they are deliberately hard to find. Vaux chose natural materials for the arches, using rough **brownstone** and sandstone blocks, bricks, and even uncut boulders, in subtle, rustic designs. His bridges, in both stone and cast iron, are sometimes **ornate**, but they, too, blend and harmonize with their surroundings, with **motifs** of flowers petals, leaves, and berries. With the exception of one **cast-iron** bridge in Pennsylvania, these are the oldest cast-iron bridges in America.

Perhaps the most famous, or at least most photographed, bridge in Central Park is the sixty-foot, cast-iron Bow Bridge (1862) spanning the Lake from the Ramble to Cherry Hill. Its iron railing was made by the same company that manufactured the **dome** of the United States Capitol. The original plans called for

one very interesting feature: cannonballs were placed inside the bridge **abutments** to act as movable ball bearings, allowing the iron bridge to expand in the heat of the summer and contract in the cold of the winter.

Of a completely different sort of beauty is Huddlestone Arch (1866). Found at the end of the Ravine in the north end of the park, it is built of boulders that were gathered from around the park, arranged to leave an almost accidental-looking passage for a stream and a footpath through the tumble of rock.

There are twenty-one arches and nine bridges throughout the park, and no two are alike. They each have their own character, and each augments the scenery in a different way. Look through one of the many arches; you will see how gracefully it frames your view. Vaux's bridges and archways are a gracious, picturesque addition to the overall landscape.

One type of road is out of sight altogether in Central Park. A park that extends for fifty-one city blocks has to allow for traffic to cut through it, but this could be noisy and disruptive, and busy intersections could be dangerous. The design solution was to sink, well below ground

level, roads that transverse the park between the east and west sides of the city. People pass over these roads on small bridges, perhaps never even noticing the steady stream of traffic until literally right on top of it. It is especially notable that Olmsted and Vaux planned these roads in the mid-1800s, when traffic wasn't nearly as loud or as dangerous as it is today.

Our eventual dependence on the automobile meant changes for Central Park. In the 1930s and 1940s, park roads were widened and straightened to facilitate these faster-moving vehicles, requiring the destruction of one cast-iron bridge and the only **marble** archway in the park. Making the park accessible to automobiles was certainly a necessity, but perhaps more sensitive planning could have avoided the loss of irreplaceable pieces of our city's history.

Of buildings and other grand constructions, there were, as we have seen, to be very few. The Arsenal (1847–51), once the New York State munitions depot and now the headquarters of the Parks and Recreation Department, and the Receiving Reservoir were incorporated into the park by Olmsted and Vaux. By prior agreement, a site was reserved for the Metropolitan Museum of Art (see pages 74–85). The park's one concession to formal public architecture was to be Bethesda Terrace (1863), a gathering place built on a grand scale. Custom dictated that there be a **promenade** for fashionable people to stroll, and this was to be the broad, tree-lined Mall (said to be the only straight line in the park's design), which serves as a stately approach to the **terrace** below. Here, a flight of steps leads down to an **arcade** that opens onto the terrace through seven stone arches, ornately carved with leaves, vines, and flowers. The arcade, its ceiling once covered with sixteen thousand Minton ceramic tiles (designed by Jacob Wrey Mould), and the two grand staircases from the carriage drive on the upper terrace combine to create an impressive, graceful entrance to the famous Bethesda Fountain, with its sculpture *Angel of the Waters,* completed by Emma Stebbins in 1873, on the shore of the Lake.

Olmsted and Vaux did welcome small structures with rural or **pastoral** associations. Many of these fell into ruin over the years, but some of Vaux's small rustic shelters have been restored. In 1979, the Dairy, one of the most charming structures in the park, was rescued from disrepair and obscurity. After years of use as a storage facility for tools and equipment, the Dairy was rediscovered and recognized as one of Calvert Vaux's original designs for the so-called "Children's District" of the park. The inviting **Gothic**-style **loggia** (an open, porch-like arcade) and **gables** give the Dairy the charm of a gingerbread house.

Built in 1869–70, the Dairy had been a popular stop for children because it actually *was* a dairy. In the days before refrigeration, milk supplied to the city by upstate farms was seldom fresh, and the milk produced in the city came from cows stabled in breweries and fed only the mash left over from brewing beer—not a very healthy diet for a milk-producing cow. The Dairy served a vital public purpose, providing good milk for sale. The shade of the airy loggia was no doubt as inviting then as it is now, and children could drink fresh milk and look out over a meadow where cows grazed.

The Dairy met Olmsted's and Vaux's conditions for a building in their park: it served a specific park purpose, while being, in an undistracting way, beautiful.

The park took many years to complete. Olmsted's role effectively ended in 1878, while Vaux continued as the main landscape architect, on and off, until his death in 1895. Meanwhile, Central Park continued to evolve, and in some cases, their ideas for the park have been overruled. Olmsted and Vaux disputed the introduction of statues and **busts** into the park, wanting to emphasize not any one individual person but rather the natural setting and the equality of all people within it. Public opinion won out, however, and between the 1860s and the present, many war memorials and commemorative statues to people, animals, and mythical figures have been erected in the park. Some of the statues fit in well with the park's landscape, because their style reflects the naturalistic and humanistic themes of the park's design. Examples include *Angel of the Waters* in Bethesda Fountain; *Indian Hunter* (1866) by John Quincy Adams Ward, southwest of the Mall; and *Still Hunt* (1883) by Edward Kemeys, of an American mountain lion perched atop a rock on the East Drive at 76th Street. But sometimes, dull statues and busts of forgotten people have ended up in the park. What disturbs the park atmosphere, and what enhances it, is of course a matter of opinion. Some statues, like *Alice in Wonderland* (1960) by José de Creeft, have become playthings, climbed on continually by children; others are virtually ignored. The designers' original intent was to have *no* statuary at all, but public taste determined differently. What do you think?

The creation of Central Park was an immense project, completed with an incredible amount of planning and effort. Even in the 1850s, when the north end of Manhattan was not covered with buildings, New Yorkers were concerned about preserving some natural areas amid a monotonous grid of straight streets, and they began to call for a great public park. It took enormous foresight to imagine how crowded with buildings and people New York City could really get, and to build a park of the size, scale, and importance of Central Park. City planning was very important then, and it is even more important now. People's needs, from highways to water supply to space for public parks, must be provided for. Such things require foresight, planning, and projection, as well as time and money. We are very lucky that the people of nineteenth-century New York had the vision and concern to create, for themselves and for future generations, the glory of Central Park; and lucky, as well, to have had sensitive leadership and staff in the New York City Department of Parks, aided since 1979 by the privately funded Central Park Conservancy, to restore and conserve it.

After Central Park was built, the appetite for parks in New York only grew. Prospect Park (1866–73) in Brooklyn was directly inspired by Central Park, and also designed by Olmsted and Vaux. They considered it their masterpiece. They also went on to design Morningside Park and Riverside Park in Manhattan, and Tompkins Park in Brooklyn. Queens, the Bronx, and Staten Island also have extensive parks. How small can a park be? In New York City, it can be as small as Samuel Paley Plaza (1967) at 3 East 53rd Street in Manhattan, a small lot that has been magically transformed into an urban oasis, with cobblestones and ivy. Here, passersby can rest and reflect in a small grove, beside a man-made waterfall, and forget for a moment the city only a few yards away.

Brooklyn Bridge

1869–1883

These days it's a quick trip by car or train across New York's East River to travel to work, to see relatives and friends, to shop, to visit a museum or go to a concert, and many people make the journey back and forth every day, and almost never by boat. There are four bridges and numerous tunnels. But before the Brooklyn Bridge was opened in 1883, the only way people crossed the East River was by ferryboat, which took anywhere from five minutes to two hours, depending on the weather. One hundred fifty years ago, water transport was a far more important part of New York's **infrastructure** than bridges, and most engineers planned the future needs of the city's transportation system in terms of larger, faster, and more numerous ferryboats. But not a German immigrant named John Augustus Roebling.

New York's infrastructure is the underlying framework of roads, bridges, tunnels, water mains, sewers, subways, and other basic networks that we depend upon constantly in our daily lives. Many discussions concerning infrastructure have been in the news recently, because many people believe America is not doing enough to maintain and improve these essential systems. The infrastructure of New York includes some of the most dramatic engineering and architectural achievements of our

Brooklyn Bridge

country's history. Planning the infrastructure of a city requires great creativity and foresight, for what you build will have to serve the needs of future generations, so it must be durable and adaptable to changing times. Roebling did this as well as anyone before or since, the one comparable achievement in New York City being Central Park (see pages 54–61).

As a student at the Royal Polytechnic Institute in Berlin, where he received his degree in engineering in 1826, John Roebling was attracted to the democracy and economic opportunities in America, and, after carefully studying possibilities for a new home, he founded Saxonburg, Pennsylvania, a German community near Pittsburgh. In 1831, he left Germany and bought a seven-thousand-acre farm there with his brother. But farming soon frustrated Roebling, and in 1837 he moved to Pittsburgh, which was the center of the expanding iron industry, to work as an engineer. There, he found himself at the center of a growing network of railroads, whose construction would require the bridging of thousands of mountain streams in the Alleghenies. In Pittsburgh, Roebling set about designing bridges and educated himself in the manufacture of iron and, eventually, of **steel**. (Steel is a commercial form of iron that is harder and stronger than **cast iron**. The special furnaces required to produce steel on a broad scale were first built in the 1850s, although it took years for steel to become widely available and for engineers to fully understand its properties. Roebling was one of the first engineers to advocate its use in bridge construction.)

Pittsburgh wasn't the only place in America in need of bridges. As New York City grew rapidly in the nineteenth century, many found re-lief from the crowding of lower Manhattan by living across the East River, in what was then the independent city of Brooklyn. Prior to 1814, small ferries, rowboats, or two-masted sailboats weathered the strong currents, fog, and ice of the East River to provide erratic transportation between Manhattan and Brooklyn. By midcentury there was fast and frequent steam ferry service between the two cities, and river crossings averaged five minutes. But even the improved ferry service was useless on winter days when extreme cold weather, ranging from zero to ten below, caused the river to freeze. At those times there was not much to be done about the ice, and a ferry could be stuck on the river for hours without moving.

Legend has it that John Roebling came to New York on a business call in January of 1852. One winter day he boarded the ferry in Manhattan with his son Washington Roebling, and on the way to Brooklyn the boat encountered icy conditions that delayed service for hours. Waiting on the ferry on that very cold day, Roebling considered whether there could be a more convenient and comfortable way to cross the river. He is said to have never forgotten that trip, and by 1856, he had prepared his first rough **plans** for a suspension bridge to cross the East River where the Queensborough Bridge is today.

John Roebling was to design many suspension bridges in the Northeast before attempting to bridge the East River, including the Delaware **Aqueduct** (1848) at Lackawaxen, Pennsylvania, which is the oldest surviving suspension bridge in the United States, and the Cincinnati Bridge (1867), which is also still in use. A **suspension bridge** is one in which the passageway is suspended from above, rather than supported from below: this is the only practical method for bridging long distances. The earliest suspension bridges consisted of two parallel ropes supporting a wooden walkway fastened at either end by a post, rock, or tree. These bridges originated in two separate alpine areas: Peru and the border between China and Tibet. The Chinese possessed a well-developed iron industry, and their bridge builders may have used **wrought-iron** chains on bridges before the Christian era.

The first modern suspension bridge was built in America in 1801, when James Finley designed and built a seventy-foot-long bridge across Jacob's Creek in Uniontown, Pennsylvania. Finley's bridge possessed the essential ingredients of a modern suspension bridge. Not only was it suspended by cables, but its **deck** was sufficiently level and rigid to carry wheeled vehicles. Such early suspension bridges were dangerous, however, and it was not until the 1840s, after the art was advanced in Europe, that American engineers experimented with long spans. It was as a student in Germany in the 1820s that Roebling first became fascinated by suspension bridges. He was to become the greatest engineer and builder of suspension bridges in the nineteenth century.

The idea for a suspension bridge to span the East River wasn't accepted right away. In 1857, Roebling wrote a letter to Congressman Abram S. Hewitt, a prominent businessman who became mayor of New York City in 1887. Roebling suggested that a bridge could stretch across the river without the need for supporting **piers** in the water to keep it from collapsing. At that time, no suspension bridge of that length had been built, and few people could envision its success. Suspension bridges did not have a dependable reputation in the eyes of the public. They were associated with many accidents and disasters in both Europe and America. In 1830, in Montrose, Scotland, many people watching a boat race from a suspension bridge drowned when one of the chains broke and the deck upon which they were standing fell into the river. The famous Menai Strait Bridge in Wales, built in 1825, was torn up by violent winds and rain during a storm in 1839. The worst accident occurred in 1850, when a whole battalion of soldiers crossing a suspension bridge in Angers, France, drowned after it collapsed beneath them.

These troubling events caused understandable resistance to the idea of building so large a bridge over such turbulent waters as the East River. Furthermore, the American Civil War, which lasted from 1861 to 1865, imposed economic pressures and distractions that interrupted planning for the bridge. It took eleven years for the idea of the bridge to be accepted. Finally, on April 16, 1867, the New York State Legislature passed an act providing for the construction of the New York and Brooklyn Bridge and establishing the New York & Brooklyn Bridge Company, and on May 23 of that year John Augustus Roebling was appointed chief engineer in charge of construction.

It's hard to believe that no one had successfully petitioned to build a bridge across the East River before 1867. The crossing between Manhattan and Brooklyn has always been one of the most heavily traveled in North America. Even before Manhattan became a city, the place where the bridge starts was used as a boarding point by Indians in canoes. On the other side of the East River there was a natural cove, at what is now Cadman Plaza (named after the Reverend S. Parkes Cadman, who was a Brooklyn pastor and a popular radio personality in 1920s America). These two landings marked the shortest distance between the two communities.

In 1638, the Dutch settlers in Manhattan bought 930 acres of land across the East River from the Canarsie Indians and called it Breuckelen (which meant "broken land") because the terrain, rather than being flat, was hilly and irregular. Farms were laid out on the land, but the farmers had to stay at inns and taverns on

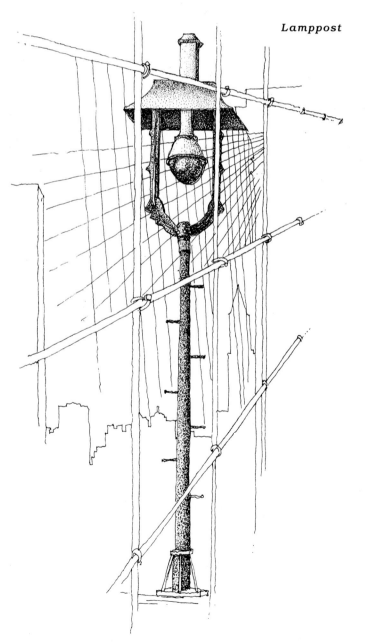

Lamppost

the southernmost tip of Manhattan until proper shelters were built on their land. Each day they would take small boats across the river and back. They did this so frequently that in 1642 a farmer named Cornelis Dircksen decided to set up a regular ferry service. The English, who captured New Amsterdam in 1664, referred to the new farmland as "Brookland," and called the ferry service the "Brookland Ferry."

One hundred sixty years after the ferry service was begun, on February 18, 1802, the New York *Evening Post* published a petition to the state legislature calling for a bridge between New York and Brooklyn. However, shipping on the East River was so important to businesses that this petition was rejected for fear that a bridge would obstruct navigation. From 1807 to 1857, at least five petitions and proposals for a bridge met the same fate. The bridge designs prior to Roebling's would have required frequent piers in the river to support the deck, and on the East River such a low bridge would have blocked shipping. But John Roebling's years of experience designing suspension bridges prepared him for the task of building a bridge that needed only two piers, one on each side of the river. Thick cables made of steel would be hung over these piers, and from these the deck would be suspended in the air, over the water, well above even the tallest ship.

Of course, what made Roebling's bridge possible was iron and steel, as well as the modern engineering skills that made it possible to plan such a complex structure. Not even Roebling would have been brilliant enough to build the Brooklyn Bridge with wood and stone. As building materials, wood and stone are very strong as weight-bearing elements, but they break easily when subjected to **tension** or other **stresses**. These natural materials are also unpredictable, because their inner structure may contain flaws, making it difficult to predict their performance under stress (which is why many old buildings that survive seem more massive than they needed to be: architects frequently overbuilt them, as a safety precaution). Iron and steel are **isotropic** materials, which means that they react identically in all directions from a given point of stress. When building with iron and steel, the engineer can use mathematics to predict the stresses on each of the many parts of a bridge and have them manufactured accordingly: as light as possible to bear the necessary stresses. The key to Roebling's success as an engineer was his mastery of the use of iron and steel. Engineering calculations such as he was able to do are now mostly done by computers!

By the time John Roebling designed the Brooklyn Bridge, he had a great deal of practice both building bridges and working with iron and steel. Early in his career he had devised the idea of replacing the old hemp ropes that the Pennsylvania Canal and Portage Railroad used to drag barges over a mountain, and which wore out and broke too often, with wire ones. Originally, his **cable** was made of iron wire twisted around in a spirallike rope, but he soon devised a second and much stronger cable. The strands of the new cable—now steel—were parallel, which meant that each individual strand could carry an identical amount of weight. This cable was so successful that it was later used in many of the most important bridges built in America in the twentieth century, including such other New York bridges as the Williamsburg Bridge (1903), the Manhattan Bridge (1909), and the George Washington Bridge (1931).

As Roebling's cable was put to more uses, a factory had to be opened to produce it in large quantities. In 1848, he bought twenty-five acres of land and built a factory called the Roebling Works in Trenton, New Jersey. Trenton was still a small town, but it was located in an industrialized area and had access to water and rail transport. Although he could have devoted his time to manufacturing his cable and other wire products, Roebling continued to focus his energies on bridges and other inventions.

It was understood in the Roebling family that John's oldest son, Washington, would follow in his father's footsteps. An 1857 graduate of engineering from the Rensselaer Polytechnic Institute in upstate New York, Colonel Washington Roebling was knowledgeable about the latest advances in steel manufacture. He was trained to oversee his father's projects, and was first assistant in the construction of the Cincinnati Bridge. This turned out to have been a fortunate circumstance. During the first year of construction of the Brooklyn Bridge, the elder Roebling's foot was crushed in an accident at the construction site, while he was doing survey work to determine the position of the bridge. Roebling, who distrusted doctors and rejected medical assistance, died in 1869 at the age of sixty-three as a result of tetanus, sometimes referred to as "lockjaw," a type of infection, caused by improperly attended wounds, that attacks the nervous system and affects the voluntary muscles. It would have been hard to find someone other than Washington to take on John Roebling's difficult job.

When he planned the bridge, John Roebling

wanted there to be four vehicular lanes: two outer lanes for horse-drawn carriages and two middle lanes for trains, pulled by cables under the roadway, which would have terminals at either end. For the cable train ride, people would have to pay five cents each time they went across the bridge. This way, he tried to ensure funding for the maintenance of his already famous bridge.

To make it possible for people to walk across the bridge during their leisure hours, a fifth lane for pedestrians was also planned. But instead of having people walk on the same level as the vehicles, he had the fifth lane suspended eleven feet above the traffic lanes. John Roebling must have known that eventually the carriages and trains would be replaced by faster vehicles, and made this decision to separate pedestrians from traffic for safety reasons. Even during his time, the volume of passenger and freight service was doubling every twelve years! You can imagine how dangerous and noisy it would be if you had to walk on the same level as cars, trucks, and trains whenever you walked between Manhattan and Brooklyn. This elevated **promenade** ensures the safety and comfort of pedestrians, separating them from the noise and exhaust of the traffic, even more than it did when the Brooklyn Bridge was new.

Because the bridge had so many lanes and was going to be so long—1,595 feet from pier to pier—and would rise so high—133 feet—above the water, its foundations needed to be very strong. It was Roebling's plan to sink the piers into the soft river bottom until they rested on the layer of solid **bedrock** on which New York is built. (Have you ever wondered why the **sky-scrapers** in New York rise so much higher

than those in other big cities? The island of Manhattan has a dense layer of bedrock close to the surface, which the foundations of sky-scrapers can grip securely enough to counter-balance their weight and height. The same principle holds true for a heavily loaded bridge.)

To support the enormous weight of the bridge, the Roeblings needed to sink the foundations of the piers deep into the riverbed, using **caissons**. These caissons were giant boxes, made of wood and iron, open at the bottom and closed at the top, that were sunk to the river bottom. They could be entered from above by climbing down spiral stairs in shafts in the **masonry** foundations and then passing through air locks that kept the compressed air in the caissons from escaping, and were large enough for as many as one hundred workers to work in, excavating the hard riverbed, once the water was pumped out of it. At the same time, workers above the ground were building the towers, so that the weight of the masonry would push the caissons deeper. This part of the project was its greatest challenge, because it required faultless execution depending on the validity of theory, design, and technical information, with no second chance for corrections in case of failure.

Although it was effective, it was also a daring and dangerous procedure that caused the injury of more than 150 workers, including Washington Roebling himself, who became permanently crippled as a result of what was called "caisson disease." In order to make it possible for people to work underwater, compressed air was used to keep water out of the caissons, and the internal air pressure increased with every inch of progress downward.

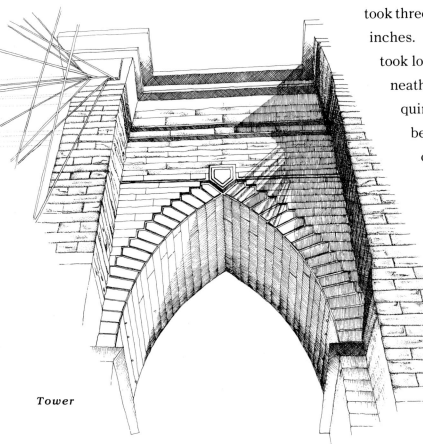

Tower

took three years to dig, and went down 78 feet 6 inches. Building the New York foundation took longer because the rock formations beneath the surface were irregular and required additional digging; it never did hit bedrock, but an examination of fossils convinced Roebling that the material that it was resting on was dense enough.

The task of excavating the foundations, sinking the caissons, and building the two main towers took over six years. Ground was broken for the Brooklyn tower foundation on January 3, 1870, and both towers were completed in July 1876. Consisting of New York **limestone** below the water and Maine **granite** above, the Brooklyn tower contained 38,214 cubic yards of stone, while the New York tower required 46,945. These towers, designed in a **Gothic Revival Style**, are both 276½ feet high and are the first aspect of the bridge that you notice, because they are so immense.

Gothic architecture emerged in France during the twelfth century and lasted until the sixteenth century. When you look at a Gothic cathedral, you can see that certain walls and doorways, as well as windows and towers, point up at the top, almost in the shape of an arrow. This special shape—a pointed rather than rounded **arch**—was developed to give the person looking at it a feeling of upward movement and vertical orientation. Don't you feel uplifted, encouraged to look upward toward the sky, while looking at a Gothic building?

From about 1835 to 1870, New York saw

Too-rapid decompression, which happened when the workers ascended quickly to the surface, caused a condition familiar to deep-sea divers called "**the bends**." Workers suffered from cramps, hearing loss, and paralysis, and three died. In order to minimize the effects of caisson disease, Washington Roebling eventually arranged for the work shifts to become shorter, but not in time to avoid health problems himself, which at several points during the construction process meant that his wife, Emily Warren Roebling, had to take over for him and supervise the construction of the bridge.

Nonetheless, the **sandhogs** (which is what the workers who dug through the sand beneath the water are called) kept on. It took a year and a half for them to hit bedrock on the Brooklyn side. The foundation there went down 44 feet 6 inches. The foundation on the New York side many structures designed in a contemporary adaptation of this style, called Gothic Revival, and the Brooklyn Bridge was one of them. John Roebling may have chosen Gothic Revival for his towers to emphasize their tremendous height and to balance the long, uninterrupted flight of the road that crosses them. Because they look like the ancient towers you would see in old cities in Europe, they give you a sense of the past. The elder Roebling had grown up in a city called Mühlhausen, an industrial town in Germany that was dominated by Gothic structures, and in the towers he paid his respects to history as well as to his own personal past, while still building a very modern and efficient American bridge.

When the two towers were completed, the next step was to hang four giant cables across them. Each of these cables measures 15¾ inches in diameter and contains 3,515 miles of wire. The roadway is suspended from these cables. In addition to the four main cables, Roebling developed a system of support cables from the towers to the deck for extra strength, and to keep the bridge deck from swaying in strong winds or storms. For this part of the construction, Roebling designed a special weaving machine that could shuttle back and forth across the East River to hang the main cables, like a spider spinning a web. The network of support cables would keep the road from collapsing even if the four main cables were somehow broken.

The massive cables that stretched from one end of the bridge to the other were fastened on each side of the river to four cast-iron plates weighing twenty-three tons each. These plates, in turn, were buried in granite **anchorages**, themselves weighing 60,000 tons each,

under the roads that led up to the bridge. Inside the anchorages were giant **vaults** made of brick and granite that ranged from one to three stories high. Usually, one keeps things of great value in a vault. This is what Washington Roebling had in mind when he planned these vaults, because he thought these spaces were secure enough to house the United States Treasury. Some of the businessmen in the area came to use these anchorages to store their goods. But when business in the area slowed down in the 1930s, they moved away and left the vaults empty.

On May 24, 1883, the Brooklyn Bridge was officially opened and dedicated with great exuberance by President Chester A. Arthur, ac-

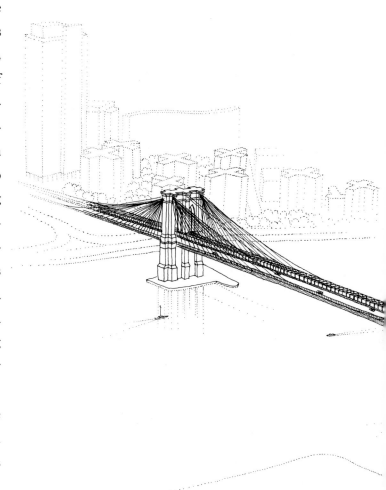

companied by Governor Grover Cleveland of New York State, Mayor Franklin Edson of New York City, Mayor Seth Low of Brooklyn, and thousands of sightseers. Everyone was there to celebrate the triumphant event—except, unfortunately, those who were truly responsible for the bridge's creation. John Augustus Roebling did not live to witness its completion, and his son Washington had sacrificed his health so severely that he had to watch the ceremony from his bedroom window overlooking the harbor in Brooklyn Heights. More than two dozen men had lost their lives during the course of construction.

On February 7, 1896, the Brooklyn Bridge survived a seventy-two-mile-per-hour gale, proving its ability to withstand windstorms. From then on, no misgivings or doubts concerning the dependability of suspension structures were expressed. However, increasingly heavy traffic over the years required that the bridge be reinforced. In 1898, heavier electric trains began to replace the cable cars, and two electric trolley tracks were added to the roadways. In 1922, it was discovered that the cables on the Manhattan side had shifted, and all motor traffic was banned from the bridge, making it available only to mass transit and pedestrians until the bridge's endurance could be determined. Washington Roebling, who was eighty-five at the time and retired, assured Mayor John F. Hylan that there was no danger, as the cables had been designed to shift in order to adjust to heavier loads. According to Roebling, the bridge could last another century. By 1950, the trains and trolleys were gone, and the roadways were widened to permit three lanes of automobile traffic in each direction.

The city of New York continues to replace parts of the bridge as they deteriorate with age, and has also said that it hopes to fill the vaults with new shops, restaurants, bookstores, and other places to enjoy when you visit lower Manhattan or the Brooklyn riverfront.

Many bridges have been erected in the world since the completion of the Brooklyn Bridge, but none has meant as much to so many areas of human activity, from engineering to art and poetry. It offered one of the first practical demonstrations of the utility of steel in construction and, almost more important, of the formidable influence of the modern engineer. Its graceful, flowing lines expressed the speed and efficiency of modern life over twenty years before the automobile entered people's lives. Its span remained the longest in the world for twenty years, when it was surpassed by the nearby Williamsburg Bridge by four feet six inches, and it was another twenty-one years before any bridge longer than these was built. But perhaps it is chiefly remarkable because it continues today to be not only as beautiful but as useful as the day it opened, nearly 110 years ago. The pedestrian lane is still open, and to walk, jog, or ride your bike across it is one of the great experiences New York has to offer.

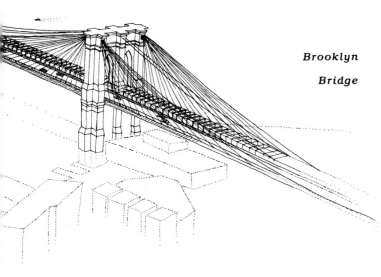

Brooklyn

Bridge

The Metropolitan Museum of Art

Begun 1874

By 1850, New York, with a population of just over half a million, was by far the largest city in North America. Baltimore, the next largest, had one-third as many people. But while New Yorkers might be proud of the growth of their city, they would have to admit that, compared to the great cities of Europe, they had a long way to go. In 1850, the population of London was over two million; of Paris, about one million.

Of course, New Yorkers might look at other measures than size alone in comparing their city to London and Paris. Beginning with ancient Athens, people have expected great cities to be centers of art and culture. New York, however, was certainly not that. Compared to Paris, for example, New York in 1850 was virtually a cultural wasteland. One obvious lack was a permanent art gallery, accessible to all persons—the kind of institution befitting a great city of commerce and civilization.

In order to address this deficiency, the lawyer and diplomat John Jay, grandson of the John Jay who was the first chief justice of the United States, proposed on July 4, 1866, to an audience of prominent American citizens and French officials gathered at a garden restaurant in the Bois de Boulogne in Paris, that they celebrate the ninetieth anniversary of the independence of the United States by helping to establish a museum and library of art in the United States. Among the guests were some

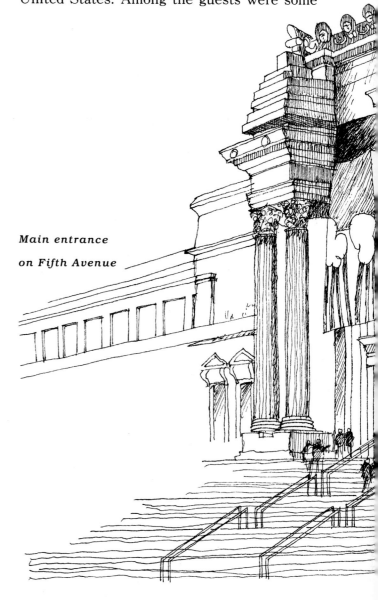

Main entrance on Fifth Avenue

73

patriotic and influential New Yorkers with the ability and ambition to help bring such an institution into existence. These gentlemen invited the Union League Club of New York, the city's third-oldest club engaged in civic, moral, and social activities, to "institute the best means for promoting" a museum of historical relics and a gallery of art for the benefit of the people. The club's art committee spent almost three years deliberating before deciding that the project was indeed worth pursuing.

The poet, orator, and editor William Cullen Bryant, New York's most prominent man of culture, presided at a meeting called by the Union League Club on November 23, 1869, of the city's leading editors, artists, lawyers, businessmen, industrialists, collectors, architects, and clergymen. Active in this enterprise was John Taylor Johnston, a man whose wealth from banking and railroads financed his passion for collecting works by living American painters. The twenty-seven-member board established by the committee appointed Johnston president of the museum on January 31, 1870, and he remained at this post for eighteen years, which comprised the earliest and most crucial stages of the museum's evolution.

The museum opened in February, 1872, in a modest **brownstone**, formerly Allen Dodworth's Dancing Academy, at 681 Fifth Avenue (since demolished), between 53rd and 54th streets. The collection consisted of 174 **old master** paintings, purchased from the industrialist William T. Blodgett, who had acquired them in Europe in 1870, when the Franco-Prussian War was forcing some collectors to sell at bargain prices; and a Roman **sarcophagus** from ancient Tarsus, donated by J. Abdo Debbas, an American vice-consul in Turkey,

that was the first gift accepted by the museum. At that time, there was not yet a museum "profession." The handful of gentlemen who volunteered to work at the museum were **amateurs** in the arts and archaeology. Visitors were left on their own when viewing the works of art, as no professional staff was there to aid them.

In 1873, the Metropolitan Museum purchased an enormous collection of more than six thousand ancient objects, which immediately created an urgent need for a newer, larger home. With this collection came, eventually, its former owner, General Luigi Palma di Cesnola, an Italian-born, self-taught archaeologist. Cesnola's diplomatic career—his brave service in the Fourth New York Cavalry Regiment in the Civil War earned him President Lincoln's appointment as American consul in Cyprus in 1865—enabled him to excavate more than sixty thousand Phoenician, Egyptian, Greek, and Roman tombs on the island before leaving for New York in 1877 with ten thousand more objects for the museum. There were statues, pottery, ceramic art, gems, gold jewelry, and glassware, which opened new perspectives on the history of ancient art and civilization. Because of his world-famous excavations and his passion for **antiquities**, as well as his military administrative experience, the trustees appointed General Cesnola as the first salaried director of the museum in 1879. For the next twenty-five years, until his death in 1904—the longest term of any director of the museum—General Cesnola made it his personal goal to make the Metropolitan Museum of Art the greatest museum in the world. His commanding presence aroused occasional antagonisms among the museum trustees and staff, but, nonetheless, he managed to rule the institution single-handedly.

With the Cesnola purchase, the second home of the Metropolitan Museum, situated at 128 West 14th Street between Sixth Avenue and Seventh Avenue in a private **mansion** that was being used as a Salvation Army Training School, overflowed with treasures. For four years, Cesnola's Cyprian antiquities and Blodgett's paintings filled every inch of space in the **mansard**-roofed mansion, while a new museum was built.

In 1872, a site had been selected by Andrew Haswell Green, a lawyer, city planner, and president of the Central Park Commission, on eighteen-and-a-half acres of land in Central Park off Fifth Avenue between 80th and 85th streets. Up to the last moment, there were those on the museum's board who would have preferred the art museum to share Manhattan Square, on Central Park West and 79th Street, with the American Museum of Natural History, and others who coveted the site of the Croton Reservoir, where the New York Public Library was soon to be built (see pages 98–107). Although it was always intended that there would be an art museum in the park, many people felt that it would intrude upon the "purity" of nature that made Central Park unique. But an innovative arrangement had been struck between the trustees and the city, which was to become a precedent for many of America's museums in the future: the city would donate the land and control the building for the museum; the trustees would control its contents. The state legislature vested the Central Park Commission with the authority to construct the museum; Green wanted it in the park, and there it went.

Calvert Vaux, who with his assistant Jacob Wrey Mould had collaborated with Frederick Law Olmsted in designing Central Park, was assigned to the museum. The construction of Vaux's and Mould's **High Victorian Gothic Style** building began in 1874. Opened to the public in April, 1880, the museum was a rectangular, red-brick structure, a building that was generally agreed to be less than beautiful, with its **axis** running from east to west. The main entrance was on the west, or park, side. High Victorian Gothic Style buildings, popular in the United States in the 1870s, are memorable for their **facades** of contrasting colors, and here the designers used bands of reddish brickwork against **limestone**. The style emphasized structure rather than ornament, which gave one the sense of solidity and timelessness that is associated with a philanthropic institution. For the interior, the museum's trustees took the advice of James Renwick, Jr., an eminent member of the staff of the Smithsonian Institution, to build a large central hall—where the glass skylight soon leaked on cases holding Cesnola's antiquities—instead of the series of long galleries that Vaux had envisioned. (For an example of a High Victorian Gothic Style building designed by Vaux, visit the Jefferson Market Branch of the New York Public Library, a designated landmark at 425 Sixth Avenue in Manhattan.)

Despite its seeming spaciousness, many works of art meant for display were still found pushed into dark corners of the museum's cellars and storerooms because there was not enough room for them in the museum. To resolve the pressing need for more space, $340,000 in funds were raised before the end of the decade to build new wings, or extensions, to the south of the main hall.

Grand
staircase

The architect-engineer Theodore Weston, who had been among the first trustees of the museum (1870–93), was commissioned to design the wings, but even as these were finished (in 1888 and 1894), the collection had already grown beyond their capacity. His additions, built in red brick in a **Renaissance Revival Style**, shifted the main entrance from the west side of the building to the south.

The most significant change came about in 1895, when America's most celebrated architect of the time, Richard Morris Hunt, created a **master plan** that was meant to bring unity to the entire structure, as well as to its relation to the site. His work formed the nucleus for the museum that we see today, at least from the Fifth Avenue side, although his master plan—that is, his vision of how the museum should expand over time—was discarded.

Richard Morris Hunt was born and raised in Brattleboro, Vermont, and attended Boston schools before being sent to a military school in Geneva, Switzerland. He went to Paris to study under and work for a French architect named Hector-Martin Lefuel in 1845, and a year later he was the first American to be admitted to the prestigious **Ecole des Beaux-Arts**, where he studied until 1855. He was so highly regarded at the school that, in 1854, he was briefly put in charge of executing Lefuel's additions to the Louvre (then considered the greatest art museum in the world). He returned to the United States in 1855 to work on additions to the United States Capitol in Washington, D.C.

Hunt's design for the Metropolitan Museum of Art achieved its majestic quality by using the **ornate** and grand-scaled vocabulary of **Beaux Arts Classicism**. The term *beaux arts*, which means "fine arts" in French, identifies not a style but a manner of decoration and crafting. The beaux arts tradition was named after the Ecole des Beaux-Arts.

The school, which was founded in 1819, is still of worldwide importance, and trains painters, sculptors, and architects. Instead of classrooms, lessons take place in *ateliers,* or studios, where students train by apprenticing themselves to masters of their discipline. The French government provided the facilities, which consisted of a large library with an enormous collection of paintings, casts, and copies of **murals**. It was difficult to become accepted as a student: in order to qualify, applicants had to pass exams and demonstrate talent in their creative work.

Hunt was only the first of many distinguished American architects who studied at the school. In this book, the New York Public Library (see pages 98–105), the U.S. Custom House (see pages 106–13), and Grand Central Terminal (see pages 114–23), in addition to the Metropolitan Museum of Art, are examples of Beaux Arts Classicism by beaux arts–trained architects. Some of the features that identify beaux arts buildings—which always use the **Classical orders**—include a strictly **symmetrical plan**; a central mass that dominates the subordinate wings; a monumental flight of steps; the use of figure sculptures, especially along the skyline; a facing of **marble** or other, more formal stone; and, oddly enough, the use of coupled, or paired, **columns** on the facade. If you look at all four beaux arts buildings mentioned above, and you can visit them all in one day by subway or car, you will find some combination of these features in each one.

Hunt's master plan included wings that extended more than fifteen hundred feet along

Fifth Avenue, which would have run from 79th Street to 85th Street. Other wings stretched all the way to the edge of the East Drive in the park. Hunt disliked Vaux's High Victorian Gothic Style, as well as the Renaissance Revival Style used by Weston. Thus, his plan "encased" the original building, concealing it from view. On the exterior of the museum, Hunt planned to use pure white marble—eighteen acres of it was necessary—to create a gleaming monument to his architectural genius.

To reconstruct the museum on a far more dramatic scale than its earlier version, Hunt gave it a new facade and set up the main entrance on a cross axis to Fifth Avenue. In this case, the visual axis from the top of the stairs happened to be 82nd Street, which did not offer an impressive **vista**, but the cross street (Fifth Avenue) did. Hunt's entrance is dominated by four pairs of coupled **Corinthian** columns, which rest upon projecting **bases** and support a broken **entablature**. On either side of this entrance were small wings of three **bays** each, which are still visible between the entrance and McKim, Mead & White's much longer wings, added later.

Unfortunately, Hunt did not live to see more than his plan for the Great Hall completed. The two-story Great Hall was constructed in 1895, to the same monumental proportions as its facade. Three saucer **domes** with circular skylights illuminate the vast space, which serves as a threshold and gathering point orienting visitors toward the sweeping, grand staircase that leads to the galleries on the second-floor level (when you climb to the top of these stairs, you are actually in Vaux's original building). The interior detailing of the Great Hall was designed by Richard Morris Hunt's son, Richard

Howland Hunt, after the senior Hunt's death in 1895, based on the unfinished sketches his father left behind as guidelines. The younger Hunt also supervised the construction of the facade, completed in 1902.

Museums built during the beaux arts era (between about 1880 and 1930) were almost always decorated with sculpture, and in the case of the Metropolitan, a Viennese artist named Karl Bitter carved the elaborate relief **portraits** in each of the **arch spandrels**. Bitter was born in Vienna, Austria, and emigrated to America at age twenty-one in 1888. The work that he became best known for was the sculpture *Pomona* of 1915, which was his last work. The bronze statue of the Goddess of Abundance, Pomona, stands atop the limestone basins of the Pulitzer Memorial Fountain, in the landmark Grand Army Plaza at 59th Street and Fifth Avenue. Unfortunately, Bitter had just finished his model for the statue on April 9, 1915, when he was hit, and killed, by an automobile while leaving the opera after an evening's entertainment. The statue had to be completed by an assistant, Isidore Konti.

The massive blocks of rough stone on the entablature, which remain uncarved to this day, were originally meant to be shaped into sculptural groups representing the arts of four great epochs in our history. The work was to be assigned to four different sculptors, but the necessary funds to complete the work were never available. Try to find the blocks when you visit the museum. Do you think they should be completed? If you could choose, what would you consider appropriate subjects for them?

This stage in the development of the museum was also the turning point between a somewhat precarious beginning and a remarkable present. If any one event ensured the future of the museum, it was the November, 1904, appointment of John Pierpont Morgan as president. Morgan was from an American banking family famous for its immense financial power and its philanthropic activities. His authority in the world of finance focused attention on the museum, setting an example for other men of affairs that art was worthy of their attention and support. He had a galvanizing effect on the museum, attracting experts to the staff and ever more powerful men to the board (women did not join the trustees until the 1950s).

Born in Hartford, Connecticut, and educated in Europe, Morgan was from early childhood exposed to great works of art and craftsmanship collected by his own family. He accumulated a magnificent art collection from his many years of travel abroad. Upon his death in 1913, his collection was valued at $68,384,680, and his son, John Pierpont Morgan, Jr., who was left all of it, donated over 5,500 objects (about 40 percent) to the Metropolitan Museum. The gift included Raphael's *Madonna and Child Enthroned, with Saints* and numerous other old-master paintings, Chinese porcelains, medieval tapestries, and other priceless objects.

Thanks to Morgan's leadership, and in no small measure due to his son's bequest, the museum was again so swollen with treasures that even the addition of six new wings was not sufficient to house the collection. These additions were designed by the celebrated architectural firm of McKim, Mead & White, one of the most prolific in the history of American architecture. The firm was responsible for helping to reestablish classically inspired architecture in the United States in the 1880s, after many years of such stylistically diverse movements as High Victorian Gothic. Like Beaux Arts Classicism, **Georgian Revival**, **Second Renaissance Revival**, and **Neoclassical Revival** buildings were intended to bring a measure of uniformity and balance back into architecture.

The firm, created by Charles Follen McKim, William Rutherford Mead, and Stanford White, was the largest and best known of its time, totaling among its commissions 350 major works, including such designated landmarks as the Henry Villard Houses (1882–86) at Madison Avenue between 50th and 51st streets and the Racquet and Tennis Club Building (1916–18) at 370 Park Avenue, two of the most significant examples of the Second Renaissance Revival in American architecture. Other designated landmarks designed by their prestigious firm are the Low Memorial Library (1895–97) at Columbia University and the James A. Farley Post Office Building (1910–15) on Eighth Avenue between 31st and 33rd streets, which reflect the grandeur of the American Neoclassical Revival of the turn of the century.

In 1904, the Building Committee of the museum commissioned McKim, Mead & White to prepare yet another master plan that would attempt to bring unity to the museum. They added two long wings on either side of Hunt's facade, which remained untouched with the exception of the front steps. These were widened to keep them in proportion with the now nine hundred feet of Fifth Avenue frontage.

The additional wings, opened in succession in 1907, 1914, and 1917, were a great success. Each was constructed in the Second Renaissance Revival Style to conform with the Great Hall. These contained the J. Pierpont Morgan collection of decorative arts, the Egyptian collection, and the Greek and Roman collection of antiquities. A garden court, currently used as the museum restaurant, was designed for Roman sculpture (plans are under way to return it to its original use).

Unfortunately, the master plan of McKim, Mead & White was ignored, as were the master plans preceding it. During the extensive construction, the museum trustees allowed the architect Grosvenor Atterbury to build the American Wing, which opened to the public on November 10, 1924. The wing was a gift to the museum from Robert W. de Forest, then the museum's fifth president. De Forest ingeniously rescued the condemned 1822 marble facade of the United States Branch Bank, formerly the old Assay Office, and had it moved from its original location on Wall Street to the museum, where he installed it in front of a collection of chronologically ordered period rooms, each filled with American furnishings and decorative objects dating from about 1670 to 1820.

This idea helped to establish an awareness of preserving valuable architectural land-

marks, and was widely imitated in other museums. The American Wing became one of the museum's most successful divisions, but it presented difficulties to the succeeding architects of the museum. Its placement was so awkward that it discouraged any hopes of attaining symmetry in the overall plan of the museum.

The next attempt to generate a master plan took place between the years 1940 and 1943, under the supervision of Francis Henry Taylor, then the museum's director. Taylor's concept was to develop a scheme whereby the museum would be divided into a series of distinct and separate "mini-museums," each specializing in the art of a distinct civilization or culture. His empathy with the confusion of the public, when faced with an overwhelming accumulation of five thousand years' worth of cultural **artifacts**, underlined problems that the museum's administration still wrestles with today.

The architect of Taylor's choice was Robert B. O'Connor, who worked closely with Aymar Embury II, an architect from the New York City parks department. Instead of focusing primarily on building a masterpiece of architecture as the previous architects in the museum's past had, they tried to solve practical problems unique to museum architecture. They needed to create a structure that ordered the vast collections in a coherent and logical way, serving the primary function of displaying art, as well as providing space for lecture rooms, offices, libraries, and storage.

But almost none of this seemingly brilliant master plan was carried out either, mostly due to the dullness of their designs and the scarcity of funds during the postwar years. The Metropolitan Museum of Art, since its founding in 1870, continued to outgrow its shell like a child outgrowing his or her clothes, without adhering to any of the well-intended plans that continually addressed the future.

By the late 1960s, the museum faced serious problems to which a well-planned solution could no longer be postponed. The galleries were no longer large enough to accommodate the thousands of visitors flowing in and out of the museum on a daily basis. The gallery spaces had not been enlarged since 1926, while the museum's attendance had increased from 1.2 million to over 4.5 million visitors a

American Wing's Engelhart Court and Assay Office facade

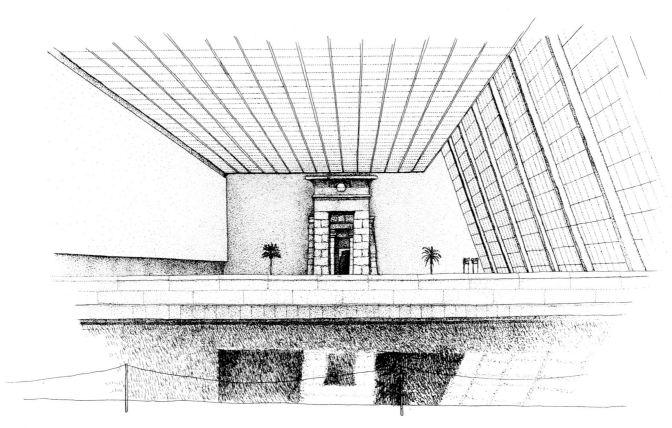

The Temple of Dendur in the Sackler Wing

year, making it the largest single tourist attraction in New York. The cluttered offices and storage spaces made it difficult to control temperature and humidity, which is essential to the conservation of precious, and fragile, objects.

At this time, the museum's board of trustees agreed upon a comprehensive master plan. Once again it was a New York City commissioner of parks, August Heckscher, who influenced the future growth of the museum: he refused to approve any new construction until such a plan was prepared. The plan was submitted by the museum's director, Thomas P. F. Hoving, who had been Heckscher's predecessor as commissioner of parks. The architecture firm selected to prepare the plan, Kevin Roche/ John Dinkeloo & Associates, spent two and a half years studying every aspect of the museum, which included the existing structure, the accumulation of recent acquisitions, staff and administrative needs, and all other requirements for a well-organized and efficient institution of art. They proposed five new wings, which would increase the museum's exhibition space by one-third. Most of the cost was to be assumed by the trustees, who agreed that the museum would not expand into the park beyond what was envisioned in this plan.

One of the first adjustments to the museum was the **renovation** of the entrance and plaza on Fifth Avenue. The original entrance had become so heavily used that there was always serious congestion at the doorway. The stairway was widened yet again, and given a series of **terraces** where visitors could sit informally on balmy days to enjoy the out-of-doors.

The architects also reorganized the galleries in a more orderly fashion, with the notion of providing a sense of progression through the history of art. Visitors were often confused by the lack of transitional spaces between galleries devoted to different subjects. Without a coherent sense of order, a museum can be overwhelming to visitors and, therefore, less effective as an educational institution or as a pleasurable experience. In keeping the arrangement of each of the museum's collections in strict chronological order, for example, starting with the earliest material first, visitors can be kept constantly aware of where they are in relation to the art that surrounds them, so that they are less likely to get "lost."

The building program actually produced not five but six new wings within eighteen years of the announcement of the comprehensive master plan in 1970. The first to be completed was the Robert Lehman Wing: a glass **pavilion** with a glass **pyramid** roof which opened in 1975. This collection, acquired in 1969 through a bequest from one of America's great art collectors, covers nearly every aspect of European art since 1300. It includes paintings, drawings, furniture, tapestries, enamels, and jewels from Italy, France, Spain, and England. In parts of the pavilion, sections of the Robert Lehman family house have been reconstructed. With this building, Roche/Dinkeloo concealed the last exposed sections of Vaux's original building behind new construction.

The Lehman Wing represented one solution (and a troublesome one, at that) to a long-term problem for the museum: people who leave great collections to the museum frequently wish them to be displayed together, while the museum's curators would almost always prefer to disperse new acquisitions throughout the museum according to where each work logically belongs. The Morgan gifts were simply added to the museum's collections, as were nearly two thousand old-master paintings, Chinese porcelains, bronzes, sculpture, and manuscripts bequeathed to the museum in 1929 by Mrs. Horace O. Havemeyer. The Havemeyer bequest included an astonishing series of works by such French Impressionists as Claude Monet and Edgar Degas. Among these works are probably some of the paintings you know and love best. The one bequest that rivaled Morgan's in quality was the Benjamin Altman collection, which came to the museum in 1913. Altman wanted his thousand or so objects displayed together, and the curators obliged this request—more or less—by exhibiting them in a meandering series of galleries, interspersed with other works. (You can find out the **provenance** of most works in a museum by noting the name of the donor on the wall labels that identify them.) A significant collection of paintings was contributed to the museum by Walter Annenberg in 1991.

The Sackler Wing, which opened in 1978, was built to house the Temple of Dendur, a 1967 gift to the United States from Egypt. This first-century-b.c. temple on the banks of the Nile River was one of five that would have been submerged in a lake that formed behind the planned Aswan High Dam. In this case, the museum had to find a way to display an entire building, rather than just an object that could fit in a display case or hang on a wall. The reconstruction of the Temple of Dendur and a suggestion of its original setting required a new and specially designed wing that would attempt to re-create the environment of the temple, as well as provide as much natural lighting as possible. The solution was a great glass building that measures 220 feet long, 130 feet wide, and 60 feet high. In this way, the architects were able to encase the temple indoors to protect its delicate stone carvings while still giving it a sense of being outdoors. The gallery also provides the viewer with the Central Park orientation that was the intent of the founders of the museum.

In 1982, the Michael C. Rockefeller Wing, with extensive galleries and a library with photographic **archives** covering the ethnographic art of Africa, Peru, Mexico, South America, the South Seas, and North America, opened. A glassed-in building similar to the Sackler Wing, it was named in honor of former New York governor and United States vice president Nelson Rockefeller's son (who died while collecting the art and culture of the Asmat people in New Guinea). Also completed in the 1980s were a total redesign of the American Wing (1980) and the Lila Acheson Wallace Wing for twentieth-century art (1987).

The final construction project in the museum's latest master plan is the Henry Kravis Wing, of which various parts have opened since 1990, that completes the Central Park facade. The new wing contains the museum's collection of European sculpture and decorative arts from the **Renaissance** through the beginning of the twentieth century. It also provides for a conservation center, where specialists can teach, research, or train others in the restoration and conservation of precious art objects.

All of the additions in the latest master plan of the museum have been made to the park side, and their acres of glass do succeed in making the visitor feel the nearness of the natural environment. But not very many seem to celebrate the view of the museum from the park. The new wings work as efficient, comfortable spaces in which to display art.

The original decision to put the museum in the park has been both a blessing and a limitation. It allowed for the growth that has now made the museum the largest in the world. How intrigued the audience at Mr. Jay's dinner in 1866 would have been to know what would come about! But unlike, for example, Paris, where limited space for new construction forced the Louvre, as its collections grew, to spawn new museums throughout the city, each with its own architectural character, the Central Park site exerted no architectural discipline. (The Cloisters, the museum of medieval art that opened in Fort Tryon Park in 1938,

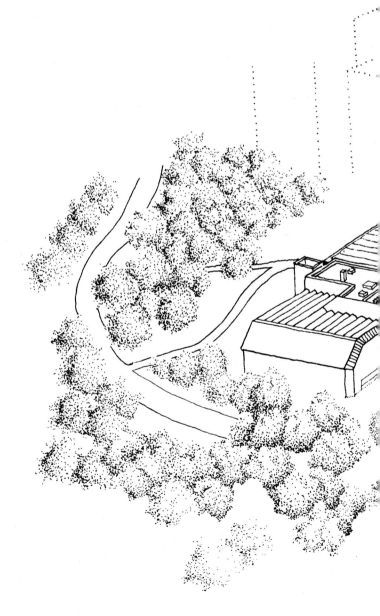

funded by John D. Rockefeller, Jr., is the only example of this kind of "satellite" growth happening at the Metropolitan Museum of Art, and it is universally believed to be a stunning achievement.) How successful is the Metropolitan Museum of Art as an architecturally unified complex of buildings? When you visit it, consider its programs, its collections, and its various styles, then you can decide for yourself.

To help guide young people who visit, the Junior Museum was established in 1941 and occupied the entire south wing on the ground floor. This area was redesigned in the early 1980s and is now known as the Ruth and Harold Uris Center for Education. It has its own special staff, which is ready to help introduce young people to the Metropolitan Museum and its many collections. You can learn about the fine and decorative arts, architecture, and design. You can even find painting sets and assembly kits to experiment with artist's materials yourself. By establishing this special section, the museum attempts to continue the principles of its founders: that the Metropolitan Museum is not only a place for the refreshment of the eye and mind, the well-being of the soul, and a treat for tourists, but a center for learning as well.

Aerial view from the Central Park side

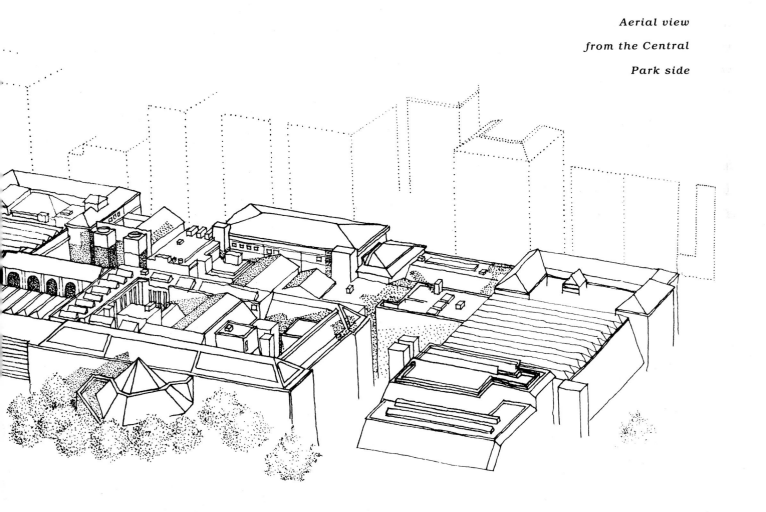

The Dakota

1880–1884

The Dakota

Many New Yorkers live in apartments, but that wasn't always the case. Before the 1880s, "home life" in New York was dramatically different from the way it is now. Then, some New Yorkers lived in boardinghouses or **tenements**, where everyone in the building shared cooking and bathing facilities. Others, who were more economically privileged, especially those with families, lived in their own houses, which, in New York City, were often town houses (see pages 38–45). But beginning in the 1880s, apartment buildings were constructed to provide the well-to-do with bright and airy residences that provided the privacy and autonomy of private houses. The first great luxury apartment building in New York City was The Dakota, opened in 1884 at 1 West 72nd Street by Edward Severin Clark, a New York lawyer and financier.

Clark made his fortune in 1854 by joining with Isaac Merrit Singer, one of the inventors of the sewing machine, to manufacture sewing machines for both private and industrial use. Their venture produced Singer Sewing Machines, which caused dramatic changes in the production of clothing, creating a new industry of standardized and ready-to-wear apparel. By the Civil War, the name Singer was synonymous with the sewing machine. Nearly every well-equipped household had one, liberating housewives from the many hours and complicated handwork formerly required to make clothes. Mass-produced ready-made clothing appeared for the first time in stores, and people could buy patterns for clothes they wanted to make for themselves at home.

By the 1870s, the shops along the Ladies' Mile (the most fashionable shopping district of the time), just north of 14th Street, offered many examples of stylish new merchandise. And just as these shops educated the taste of customers to what was considered new and fashionable in clothing, Clark's idea for a fresh approach to city dwelling helped shape New York City, because it filled a need for elegant, and convenient, urban living.

Located on what is now 72nd Street and Central Park West, The Dakota, at the time of its construction, was so far removed from the center of New York City that people joked about it as being in "Dakota Territory," meaning that it was as remote as the Dakotas (in the still largely unknown western part of the North American continent), and not to be taken seriously as a desirable place to live. Furthermore, those who could afford their own houses considered it undignified to live under the same roof with unrelated families. In anticipation of its failure, skeptical people referred to it as "Clark's Folly." You would think that this kind of public reaction would have discouraged Clark, but he decided to capitalize on it, and to turn the negative talk into an asset. He remained undeterred in his determination to have his apartment house. He named it "The Dakota," and decorated it with images evoking the Old West, including a carved Indian head (over the main entrance), molded arrowheads, and sheaves of wheat.

Nothing tangible seemed to point to The Dakota as a practical alternative to existing New York housing. Clark envisioned the "West End" as a magnificent new section of the city. He dismissed the warnings of **real-estate developers** that the Upper West Side was the cheap side of town because it was isolated from the East Side and the bustling city center in lower Manhattan. He hoped to add a dimension of **diversity** to the city's residential neighborhoods, and he felt that The Dakota could help to establish a new section of the city that would combine apartment buildings with single-family town houses. He envisaged a neighborhood where people of varying economic resources could coexist, all at a reasonable level of comfort. Although the wealthy, who were accustomed to living in strictly private residences, would initially balk at the idea of living in apartments, he believed that it was only a matter of time before the new lifestyle would catch on.

Two major technological advances—the elevator and the **el**—helped to ensure the success of The Dakota. In 1852, Elisha G. Otis, a Yonkers mechanic, invented the first safety passenger elevator, which was installed in the E. V. Haughwout Building, at the corner of Broadway and Broome Street, in 1856 (see pages 46–53). The elevator made it possible to build over five stories, but until the late 1870s its cost discouraged its use in residential buildings. By the early 1880s, when The Dakota was planned, the elevator was becoming more of a fact of New York's daily life. In the years to follow, Otis elevators were installed in most of New York's multistoried buildings, and Otis's two sons marketed the company's products internationally. (The next time you are in an elevator, why not take a moment to see who has manufactured it.)

By the late 1870s, it was possible to ride uptown on Sixth or Ninth Avenue on the el. You could take the Metropolitan Elevated Railway, a privately owned steam railroad, from Trinity Church, at Broadway and Wall Street, up Sixth Avenue to 58th Street in sixteen minutes! The el ran above ground level, on raised tracks, so that it did not take up space on the busy city streets. Clark was counting on the fact that the stations on the Ninth Avenue line, one block to the west of The Dakota, would provide a suitable means of transportation between Manhattan's business districts and the residential neighborhood that Clark wanted to establish.

Clark purchased the land for The Dakota when the area was still a mass of cheap tenements and shanties and Central Park was not yet completed. In addition to The Dakota, he would build twenty-seven **row houses** on West 73rd Street between Eighth and Ninth avenues, all of which would rely for their electricity on a power plant in the basement of The Dakota. The site was one of the highest in the city and overlooked much of Manhattan, as well as Long Island Sound and Brooklyn to the east, and the Hudson River and the Palisades to the west. The residents of The Dakota would be afforded these picturesque views, with Central Park just a walk away if they desired the peace, and refreshment, of nature.

The distinguished New York architect Henry J. Hardenbergh, whose 1879 Vancorlear Hotel at Seventh Avenue and 55th Street (since demolished) had sparked Clark's interest, was commissioned to design The Dakota and the twenty-seven row houses alongside it. As in all of Hardenbergh's work, including the Plaza Hotel on 59th Street and Fifth Avenue, which he went on to design in 1907, Hardenbergh based his designs on various **Renaissance** forms, achieving a brilliant balance of styles that mirrored the **eclecticism** of the times.

Clark allotted an impressive $2 million for the construction of The Dakota, which took four years to build. This generous budget made possible a massive structure approximately

*Rooftop dome
and dormers*

two hundred feet wide and deep that was completely fireproof and lavishly decorated. Most notable for its time was the fact that there were elevators at each of the four corners, so that tenants could go directly to their own living quarters without having to pass through a main lobby, a feature that was thought to be particularly appealing to tenants, in contrast to buildings where one was forced to encounter neighbors on a daily basis.

For the exterior of The Dakota, Hardenbergh chose materials of soft, pale hues to balance the darkened areas created by the shadows of windows, **cornices**, and balconies. The building's **facade**, when it is clean, is very colorful. It was made from a newly invented buff-colored brick (perfected in 1883 by the brickmakers Sayre and Fisher), whose manufacture required a special process to remove the iron content that produces the reddish col-

or of ordinary brick. These were highlighted with olive sandstone trim and **terra-cotta** ornament.

Viewed from a distance, with its facades topped by **mansard** roofs bearing a splendid array of **dormers**, chimneys, **finials**, and **crestings**, The Dakota has a lively and deceptively lightweight appearance. The irregular exterior made it possible for residents to point out their own particular set of windows and decoration, allowing for a sense of separateness from what was still considered a rather uncomfortably large and unified whole.

The busy facades are organized horizontally and vertically into three sections. The vertical sections are the **base**, consisting of the basement and the first two stories; the four-story **shaft**; and the roof. The divisions between the sections are clearly marked: a wide band with carved panels separates the base from the shaft; an extended **balcony** with metal railings divides the shaft from the roof. **Bays** divide the building into vertical sections. The bays are detailed with such delightful elements as seven-story rounded **oriels** topped by **domes**.

The main entrance is a two-story archway, or **arch**-covered passageway, opening at 72nd Street, which was large enough for the carriages that brought supplies and deliveries to the building. Iron gates led to a **groin-vaulted vestibule**, with a second set of iron gates opening into an enormous I-shaped **courtyard**, with sparkling fountains, for horse-drawn carriages. Now that trucks and cars have replaced the carriages, the courtyard no longer admits motor vehicles because it cannot sustain the increased weight.

This courtyard, based on traditional Mediterranean residential design, not only gave residents a sense of seclusion from the city but served the practical function of bringing light and air to rooms on the inside of the building. A report of 1883 claimed that tall buildings constituted a health hazard, because sunlight (which limited the presence of disease-breeding germs) was blocked from the lower floors of apartment houses. The courtyard successfully solved this problem by creating a "well" of sunlight that flooded the interior rooms.

Surrounding the building, a **moat**, bordered by an iron fence decorated with sea gods and sea urchins, playfully called attention to The Dakota's secluded location. Clark successfully turned what was seen as a disadvantage into a desirable quality: he promoted The Dakota as a peaceful retreat from the chaotic city center. With exterior walls almost twenty-eight inches thick, it is still one of the quietest buildings in New York City. The floors are three feet thick, constructed with alternating layers of brick and mud from Central Park. This added **insulation** helps keep the building cool in the summer and warm in the winter.

The Dakota provided families with the space and amenities they would have had in their own houses, and with nearly as much privacy. The original eighty-five apartments varied in size from four to twenty separate rooms. The ceilings on the first floor were fifteen feet high, and though they became slightly reduced higher up in the building, the top-floor ceilings measured a still ample twelve feet. Fine woods such as mahogany and oak were used to panel and **wainscot** libraries, reception rooms, and dining rooms. Other details included **parquet** floors, fireplaces with tile **hearths**, **mantels** with mirrored **overmantels**, and carved **buffets**. Nearly every room was equipped with a wood-burning fireplace. Elegant furnishings, such as **porcelain** bathtubs in the spacious bathrooms and **marble** in the kitchens, gave utility rooms a sense of luxury as well.

Original tenants of The Dakota were provided with croquet lawns and tennis courts, private gardens, and stables, which were located in a three-story building on the southeast corner of 75th Street and Broadway. There was a wine cellar in the basement, in addition to storerooms, a bakery, a laundry, and a kitchen. For transient lodgers, an elegant dining room with a spectacular view of Central Park was built on the ground floor. This dining room served permanent residents of the building as well, offering an alternative to the home-cooked food served in their own dining rooms.

Since the notion that "the higher the floor, the more desirable the apartment" had not yet gained popularity, all the servants' quarters were located on the top two floors of The Dakota. These quarters had the most splendid views in the entire building. Located just beneath the mansard roof were laundries and drying rooms, and a playroom and gymnasium for the children of residents. (They have since been converted to residential apartments.)

The Dakota attracted many well-known people of wealth and prestige, including the music publisher Gustave Schirmer, the piano maker Christian Steinway, and the educator John A. Browning. The building was such a success that it was already fully rented by the time it opened in 1884, and people who desired an apartment had to put their names on a waiting list until a vacancy came up. Recent research reveals that, in spite of the many jokes made at Clark's expense about the remoteness of the building's site, a majority of its first tenants were already living north of 44th Street when they moved to The Dakota.

The success of The Dakota helped to change the living arrangements of New Yorkers, who soon adjusted to the idea of apartment life. Before long, imitations sporting similar names appeared on the scene. There was the Nevada at 69th Street and Broadway, the Yosemite at 62nd Street and Park Avenue, the Montana at 52nd Street and Park Avenue, and the Wyoming at 55th Street and Seventh Avenue (all since demolished). Unfortunately, Clark died two years before the completion of The Dakota, leaving the building to his twelve-year-old grandson, who also inherited the eighteen-room apartment of his grandfather.

The Dakota, the first great apartment house in New York City, has been favored by creative people from the worlds of music and the stage, and counts among its past and present residents Leonard Bernstein, John Lennon and Yoko Ono, Judy Garland, Lauren Bacall, and Rudolf Nureyev.

Ornate railing
around the moat

Carnegie Hall

1889–1891

Carnegie

Hall

There is an old joke that begins with someone asking directions at a street corner: "How do you get to Carnegie Hall?" "Practice, practice," answers a passerby. It is true that only the most gifted musicians can hope to play at Carnegie Hall, one of the world's most celebrated music halls and—at 57th Street and Seventh Avenue—not hard to get to at all.

Today, New York City is generally considered the cultural capital of the world, and institutions like Carnegie Hall helped to make it so. From the 1850s to the 1870s theaters were downtown, clustered in little groups around lower Broadway, the Bowery, and Union Square. The heart of the city was in lower Manhattan, and uptown was largely unsettled, with acres of undeveloped land. It was not until the 1870s that theaters appeared uptown along Broadway, north of Madison Square at 23rd Street. This cultural expansion was in part the result of the construction of the **el**, which by the late 1870s carried passengers between the Battery and midtown. People were more inclined to live uptown if they had access to rapid, reliable transportation, and in turn the increased population supported the building of theaters, concert halls, and museums. Furthermore, improved transportation made it possible for New Yorkers to travel much farther for pleasure; by the end of the century, it was an easy trip to Coney Island in Brooklyn or the Bronx Zoo.

The important concert halls in New York City in the 1880s included the Academy of Music at Irving Place and 14th Street and the original Metropolitan Opera House at Broadway and 39th Street (both demolished). The opera house was built in 1883, paid for by wealthy New Yorkers who were angry at having been denied the chance to buy luxury viewing boxes (a bit like those found in athletic stadiums today) at the older Academy of Music. Still, New York City was clearly short of adequate concert halls for live musical performances.

The history of Carnegie Hall actually begins with an orchestra conductor named Leopold Damrosch, who came to New York City from Germany in 1871. Damrosch was one of the small group of people who worked to increase the number of places to hear music in the brave new world of the United States. Between 1873 and 1877, he helped form the New York Oratorio Society and the New York Symphony; the latter merged with the older New York Philharmonic in 1928. These groups performed at various halls around Manhattan, but neither of them had a permanent home in the city. In 1885, Damrosch died without fulfilling his desire to have that concert hall built, but his twenty-three-year-old son, Walter Damrosch, took up the challenge.

After his father's death, Walter became the conductor of both the Oratorio Society and the New York Symphony. Through these groups he came in contact with both musicians and **patrons** dedicated to the development of music in the United States.

One of those dedicated people was Louise Whitfield, a member of the Oratorio Society and the fiancée of Andrew Carnegie. Carnegie was a member of the board of the Oratorio Society, as well as one of the richest men in the world. In 1887, Walter Damrosch and the Carnegies (by then married) took the same ship to Europe—Damrosch was going to Germany to study music, and the Carnegies were on their honeymoon trip to Andrew Carnegie's native Scotland. During the voyage, the Carnegies invited Damrosch to visit them in Scotland after his studies were completed. Damrosch did just that, and seized the opportunity to convince Andrew Carnegie to support the construction of a new music hall in New York City.

Carnegie, born in Dunfermline, Scotland, in 1835, was a self-made man. (In reality, isn't everyone—man or woman—*self*-made?) At the age of thirteen, he came with his family to America, where his father, who was a weaver, hoped to find work. The family settled in Allegheny County, Pennsylvania, and Andrew got a job as a bobbin boy at the Blackstock Cotton Mill for $1.20 per week. Soon after, he became a telegraph boy, which by 1859 led to employment as a superintendent of the expanding Pennsylvania Railroad.

By the 1860s, Carnegie had saved enough money to invest in iron manufacturing, and in the 1870s—recognizing America's need for **steel**—he started to buy up companies that he would later consolidate into the Carnegie Steel Company. By 1900, his company was making 25 percent of the steel in the United States and controlled important segments of the associated industries of railroads, ore ships, iron mines, and coke ovens. In 1901, Carnegie sold his empire to the United States Steel Corporation for the then huge sum of $250 million and retired from the steel business. After that, he concentrated on administering his fortune, which grew steadily through investments, and donating large amounts of money to various causes for the public good.

Carnegie knew exactly how he wanted to handle his fortune. He sincerely believed that a wealthy man had special duties and responsibilities: to live modestly, to provide for the needs of the people who are dependent upon

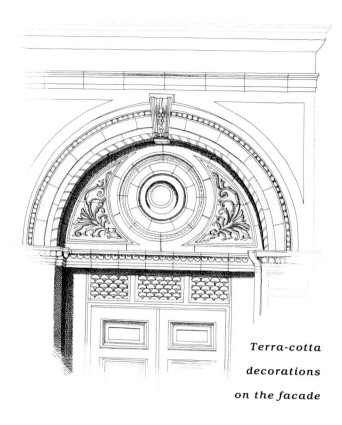

Terra-cotta decorations on the facade

him, and to devote whatever funds are left over after that to the good of society. By the time of his meeting with Walter Damrosch in 1887, Carnegie had begun a program of **philanthropy** that would expend $325 million of his fortune by 1919, the year of his death.

In 1889, Carnegie formed a **corporation** to build the hall that was supposed to be named the Music Hall Company of New York, Limited. He had hoped to finance the original construction of the building and then have the community support its costs of operation. Much to his dismay, the hall continually produced a deficit rather than a profit, and Carnegie was forced to absorb the losses himself. This shortfall of revenue continued to plague the hall for many decades.

The land that Carnegie selected for the new hall was far from the entertainment centers of lower Broadway. Instead, it was located on the Cosine Farm, at the foot of Goat Hill, uptown in the area that is now the West 50s. The new hall would be surrounded by the **mansions** of wealthy New York families—the Rockefellers, Guggenheims, and Vanderbilts, for example. As for the Carnegies, they also lived in the area, having bought a mansion on West 51st Street, which they would later give up for an even grander one on Fifth Avenue at 91st Street (now the Cooper-Hewitt Museum) at the turn of the century. The area around the future site of the hall was still only sparsely settled. A visitor to the neighborhood could admire the great houses of the rich or stroll in the wilds of Central Park. Carnegie may have chosen this uptown location for the hall in order to accommodate both himself and his affluent neighbors, who would, he hoped, become the hall's core audience.

William Burnet Tuthill, a member of the board of the Oratorio Society, was selected as the architect of the building. Tuthill had a strong interest in **acoustics**—he was a popular lecturer on the subject. Both Andrew Carnegie and Walter Damrosch considered this important, because they wanted to build a hall that would enhance (rather than distort) a live musical performance.

Ironically, even though its patron Andrew Carnegie made a great deal of his money from the iron and steel business, Carnegie Hall was one of the last significant buildings in New York City to use a framework of **terra-cotta** brick and concrete without interior reinforcements of iron or steel. As time went on, the use of steel would become widespread, and permit the construction of soaring **skyscrapers**.

Tuthill built Carnegie Hall in the **Renaissance Revival Style**. The building, including its fifteen-story tower, was clad in reddish brown brick, with **arches**, **pilasters**, **belt courses**, and terra-cotta decorations. The **masonry** walls were an imposing four feet thick so they could bear the heavy structural load.

The result of the extensive detailing and ornamentation is that externally, Carnegie Hall has a very complex design—the eye has a lot of things to examine at every level of the building. Inside, however, there is less ornament, and, in the main concert hall, the elegant sweep of the auditorium's lines is given full emphasis. The interior colors added to the serene atmosphere, through Tuthill's choice of a cool rose tint for most of the walls, as well as creamy yellow with white accents for the pilasters.

Carnegie Hall really has three different sections that were interconnected to create one building: a main hall, a recital hall with practice studios, and more studios and offices in a third section that runs along the back of the building. The structure was originally covered by a **mansard** roof, which was removed in 1894, when construction began on a floor of studio spaces as well as a tower of studios along the 56th Street side of the building. The financial success of these additions prompted the construction of another tower of studios along east side of the building in 1896. While Tuthill understood Carnegie's financial motive for wanting to increase the size of Carnegie Hall, he felt that any additions would destroy the integrity of his design and refused to be involved. Carnegie hired the architect Henry J. Hardenbergh to design the two towers.

The most impressive aspect of Carnegie Hall, however, was its acoustics. William Tuthill designed the hall to fully serve its musical needs. In order to get the best sound possible, the boxes of the main hall's balconies facing the stage had elliptically curved fronts and the elliptical ceiling was flat instead of being a **dome**. These gently rounded spaces eliminated sharp angles and edges that would have created a bouncing, reverberating sound.

Velvet was installed on the seats because Tuthill knew that it would absorb sound, which would otherwise be deflected off the hard surfaces in all different directions. The hall's dramatic sweep and sight lines (unblocked by thick support pillars) were made possible through the use of a system of brick arches and **cast-iron** posts under the stage. The first curtain was probably installed about 1915 to create a more intimate setting for chamber music concerts. Because of Tuthill's ingenuity, New York City was given an acoustically brilliant concert hall that would become known throughout the world.

Tuthill also made sure that the practice studios—all one hundred and seventy of them—benefited from his acoustical knowledge. The walls of the studios were built of masonry four feet thick, and musicians could practice without fear of bothering each other. Over time, the studios were altered to suit the needs of particular musicians. For example, the organist of St. Patrick's Cathedral, Pietro Yan, installed a fourteen-stop organ that he could practice on without having to worry that he would be disturbing anyone in the surrounding studios.

Although construction of Carnegie Hall would continue through 1897, the grand opening of the hall—still known simply as the Music Hall—was held as soon as it was possible, on May 5, 1891, with a gala event that lasted over five days. The great cost and awe-inspiring specifications of the building ($1.25 million; 3,000 seats; 4,000 electric lamps) captured the interest of New York's thirty-odd newspapers, which ran numerous articles on the subject. The featured guest conductor, the great Russian composer Pyotr Ilich Tchaikovsky (who was to conduct some of his own works for the occasion), cried from apprehension in his hotel room before the event. At 8:00 P.M. Walter Damrosch strode onto the stage, bowed to Andrew Carnegie and the rest of the public, and began the program. William Tuthill was not present because he had come in earlier, taken one look at the crush of people on the **balcony**, and turned white with terror at the thought that the supports would not hold. He rushed home to check his mathematics, sure that he had made a mistake. After an hour-long speech by Bishop Henry Codman Potter of the Episcopal diocese of New York, Damrosch and Tchaikov-

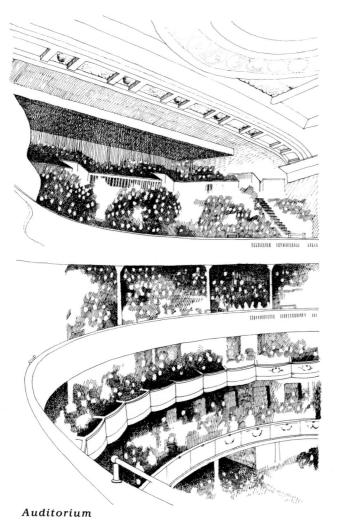

Auditorium

sky took over, and the musical part of the program was a great success. Carnegie Hall had become a part of New York City.

The legendary role Carnegie Hall was to play in establishing the reputations of musicians began soon afterward, with the performances of the young Polish pianist Ignacy Jan Paderewski, in November of 1891, when excited audiences rushed the stage. The hall was host to every type of cultural event—short of theater—from dance recitals and comedy evenings to political debates and lectures. It was home to the New York Philharmonic from 1892 to 1962, when the orchestra moved to Lincoln Center. But it was best known for those magical evenings when a visiting musical star of the first magnitude, be it instrumental virtuoso or popular singer, beguiled New York. The hall would fill, the lights would go down, and many a New Yorker would be treated to the musical experience of a lifetime.

However, even legends age, and, by its eighty-fifth birthday in 1976, Carnegie Hall was facing grave problems. Inspired and led by the distinguished violinist Isaac Stern, the trustees of Carnegie Hall asked the architectural firm of James Stewart Polshek and Partners to evaluate the hall's condition, and the fund-raising needed to pay for the work began. It took a heroic effort, but in the end some $60 million was raised. The renovation produced a new maple-wood stage, a new floor, and new plush red seats. The four-foot-thick masonry walls were replastered, the gold detailings were redone, and the ushers were given striking new uniforms designed by Ralph Lauren.

Carnegie Hall reopened on December 15, 1986, with a performance featuring the New York Philharmonic. The great question was, of

Ticket windows

course, how the renovation had affected the hall's superb sound. The reports after the concert were mostly enthusiastic, although inevitably there were complaints that the legendary acoustics of years past had been destroyed.

After the reopening it was only a short time before Carnegie Hall celebrated its one hundredth birthday. The Centennial Gala of May 5, 1991, was another grand affair, and some of the most celebrated names in music performed, from such singers as the tenor Placido Domingo and the soprano Leontyne Price to the cellists Mstislav Rostropovich and Yo-Yo Ma. The Centennial Gala was a fitting tribute to Carnegie Hall's first hundred years, a promise to the next century.

The New York
Public Library

1902–1911

Main entrance

on Fifth Avenue

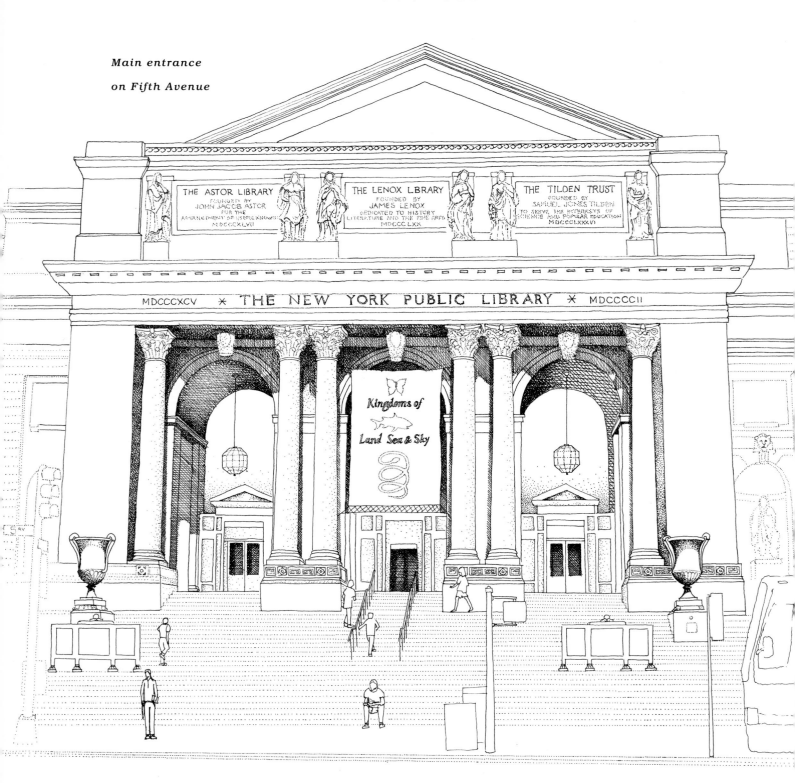

New York City produced what seems like an inexhaustible amount of wealth in the nineteenth century, and much of it appeared to find its way into the pockets of a relatively small number of individuals. It was a sense of civic responsibility and public spirit that motivated some of these men—and they *were* all men—to provide cultural institutions worthy of an emerging world-class city. Given their interests, it was probably inevitable that New York would have great museums like the Metropolitan Museum of Art (see pages 74–85) and concert halls like Carnegie Hall (see pages 92–97). It is far less predictable that private wealth would support a great public library, for if any single building in New York could be referred to as "the people's palace," it would be the New York Public Library. Grand in scale, profuse in detail, and noble in function, it has been an impressive presence on Fifth Avenue between 40th and 42nd streets since 1911. This monumental structure has a monumental purpose—to hold one of the greatest collections of knowledge in the world, and to make that knowledge freely available to all.

In nineteenth-century New York City, three rich and powerful men—John Jacob Astor, James Lenox, and Samuel J. Tilden—all had the determination, the power, and the money to create substantial libraries. Before they died, Astor and Lenox both founded small libraries in their names, and Tilden left money in his will for the same purpose. The ideas, book collections, and **philanthropy** of these three became the basis upon which today's library was built. That is why the library's official name is "The New York Public Library, Astor, Lenox and Tilden Foundations."

What is unusual about these three men coming together to create a library is that none of them was alive when its planning began. John Jacob Astor was, in the 1830s, the nation's richest man. Astor Place in Manhattan and the community of Astoria in Queens were named after him. So was the Waldorf-Astoria Hotel at 301 Park Avenue at 50th Street, as well as the town of Astoria, Oregon, outside of Portland, where he once had a fur-trading post. Originally from Germany, Astor made a great fortune in the United States as a fur merchant, shipowner, and real-estate investor. His only philanthropic act was to endow New York's first free library. He died in 1848, but his splendid general reference collection, which emphasized literature and American history, opened as the small Astor Library at 425 Lafayette Street in 1852. Unfortunately, this library was open only from 10:00 A.M. to 4:00 P.M., making it virtually impossible for anyone who had to work for a living to use the facility. (The Astor Library building was purchased by the Hebrew Immigrant Aid Society in 1920, but by 1965 it was facing demolition. The building was saved by the imagination and determination of the New York Shakespeare Festival's director, Joseph Papp, who persuaded the city to buy it so that it could become a public theater. In 1991, when Papp died, the structure, now a designated landmark, was renamed the Joseph Papp Theater in his honor.)

You might recognize the name of James Lenox from Manhattan's Lenox Avenue, Lenox Hill Hospital, and Lenox Hill neighborhood. There is also Lenox Road in Brooklyn. A philanthropist and **bibliophile**, Lenox founded a small library in 1870, ten years before his death. The Lenox Library, on Fifth Avenue and 70th Street (where Henry Clay Frick later built a **mansion**, now a designated landmark and the home of one of the finest small museums in the world, the Frick Collection), held a very special collection of rare books, manuscripts, and American artworks, including a Gutenberg Bible of 1455, the first book printed with movable type. (Today, you can see this Bible on display in the Gottesman Exhibition Hall on the New York Public Library's main floor.)

What actually led to the creation of the New York Public Library was the last will and testament of the third man, Samuel J. Tilden. Tilden was a distinguished railroad attorney and governor of New York from 1875 to 1877. In 1876, he ran for president of the United States, only to be defeated by Rutherford B. Hayes in a controversial election. (Tilden won the popular vote, but a partisan committee awarded Hayes all the disputed electoral votes and thereby, the election.) When Tilden died in 1886, he left twenty thousand books and four million dollars (a great deal of money, then as well as now) to establish a new, *public* library. His relatives contested his will, and the four million dollars that had been left for the library was reduced by half. The Tilden Trust, as these books and money were called, was no longer enough to establish a new library of the size or importance Tilden had envisioned. But if the resources of the trust were combined with another small library, there could perhaps be one truly great collection. The trustees (the custodians of Tilden's books and money) sought a way to combine these resources with others, to see if they would indeed be able to carry out Tilden's wishes.

And so it came about that in 1895, the Astor Library, Lenox Library, and Tilden Trust came together to create the New York Public Library, merging three good private collections into one great public one. It was decided then that the new library would stand in a convenient, central location in Manhattan, and that it would be open every day, from early in the morning until well after dark, with all of its contents available to anyone, simply for the asking.

Six years later, in 1901, Andrew Carnegie gave the city $5.2 million to establish a **branch library** system, to give people access to books in their neighborhoods. Sixty-five libraries were built with Carnegie money, of which four, all in Manhattan, are designated New York City landmarks: Yorkville Branch (1902) at 222 East 79th Street; West 135th Street Branch (1904–5, now part of the adjacent Schomburg Center for Research in Black Culture) at 103 West 135th Street; Hamilton Grange Branch (1905–6) at 503–505 West 145th Street; and 115th Street Branch (1907–8) at 203 West 115th Street. A fifth landmark library, the Ottendorfer Branch (1883–84) at 135 Second Avenue, is the oldest branch library in Manhattan, and predates Carnegie's bequest.

In 1897, a site not far from Grand Central Terminal was chosen for the new library, the only problem being that the land was already occupied by the city's water reservoir, called the Croton Reservoir. The reservoir and its small adjoining park, at Fifth Avenue and 42nd Street, covered the entire area where the library is today. People picnicked and even fished there! The city government agreed that this would be an ideal place for the new library, and so permission was given to remove the reservoir, although the system that brought water to the city from Lake Croton in northern Westchester, of which it was a part, continued to be an important source of New York's drinking water. (Another reservoir in the system is in Central Park, see pages 54–61.) The architects who built the library were able to use the reservoir foundations for the new building. Since it is built on city land, the city maintains and preserves the library building itself. But the library itself is a private institution, and its research facilities are maintained and supported by private contributions and endowments. The small park behind the library is called Bryant Park, named for William Cullen Bryant, who was instrumental in founding the Metropolitan Museum of Art. (This park was extensively restored in 1991 under the auspices of the Bryant Park Redevelopment Corporation.)

Just after the Astor, Lenox, and Tilden merger, in December of 1895, the library named its first director. Dr. John Shaw Billings was a very accomplished man: he had been a surgeon with the Union Army during the Civil War, he was a professor and director of the University Hospital at the University of Pennsylvania, and he even designed hospitals, such as Johns Hopkins Hospital in Baltimore. He came to his post as director of the New York Public Library with enthusiasm, as well as some very strong ideas about the design of the building. He emphasized the building's function, demanding efficient book storage and retrieval, as well as large, light, and quiet reading rooms. He even prepared a **floor plan** and suggested economical building materials, such as **limestone** or brick. By the time a **design competition** for the library was announced in May, 1897, Billings's ideas for the building were well known. The competitors were not required to follow his suggestions, but, as Billings's pencil sketch still exists, we can see that most entries, including the winning one, followed his guidelines rather closely.

The design competition was open to anyone, although New York's most famous, established architectural firms were specifically invited to submit **plans**. Third place went to the renowned firm of McKim, Mead & White; second, to a smaller firm called Howard & Cauldwell, which had not been one of the firms specifically invited. The winner was a relatively young firm called Carrère & Hastings. The cornerstone was laid in 1902.

The architects John Carrère and Thomas Hastings (both former **draftsmen** for McKim, Mead & White) and their team of about twenty men ultimately produced ten thousand sketch-

Aerial view

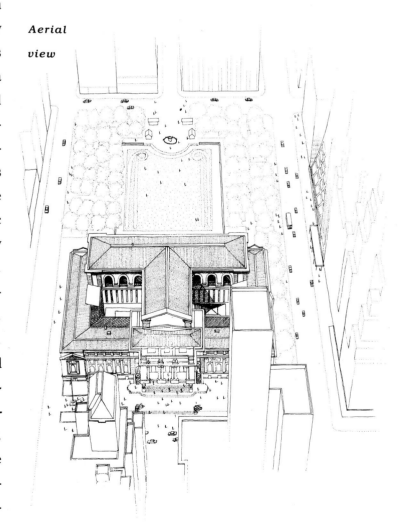

es and six thousand detailed drawings for their library design. They are responsible for envisioning almost every detail you see in the library, large and small. They designed the impressive exterior of the library, with the three large **porticoes**, the **columns** and statues, and the expanse of white **marble**. They designed all the ornamental detailing you see throughout the building, the sculpted creatures, scrolls, and **rosettes**, the intricate ironwork and beautifully inlaid woods. They even designed all of the interior furnishings: lamps, tables, chairs, doorknobs, light fixtures, drinking fountains, clocks, exhibition stands and cases, and even wastepaper baskets and step stools.

Each architectural design, once drawn, went to a modeler, who worked it up three-dimensionally in plaster. If the architects liked the plaster model, the design would be duplicated by artisans, such as wood carvers, stone carvers, or **stucco** workers, in the proper material. Other workers carved and shaped the vast amount of marble in the building, piece by piece, in the marble-cutting yards of Long Island City. Think how unfortunate it is that all of these immensely skilled craftspeople, mostly German and Italian immigrants, go unnamed, and that their crafts had almost been lost. Today, there is a revival of interest in such crafts. The Cathedral of St. John the Divine, Amsterdam Avenue and 112th Street in Manhattan, now operates a stone-cutting school and factory, training artisans, many of whom come from the area surrounding it.

The library is huge—it is two city blocks in length—and sits upon a broad stone **terrace**. In this way, raised above and away from the bustle and noise of Fifth Avenue, the library

Astor Hall

maintains an enduring sense of dignity and importance. The entire **facade** of the structure is white marble a solid foot thick, brought in exclusively from two quarries in Vermont, and now weathered to a warm, pearly shade of gray. In fact, Carrère & Hastings overruled Billings's request for somber, economical building materials, and insisted that only the elegance of marble would do. An extravagant amount of marble was used to construct the New York Public Library, both inside and outside: all in all, twenty-three different kinds in fourteen different colors. Marble for the library was shipped from no fewer than six states (Connecticut, Tennessee, Massachusetts, Vermont, Pennsylvania, and elsewhere in New York) and five foreign countries (Italy, France, Greece, Germany, and Belgium). One type of stone in the library was also used for the base of the Statue of Liberty; another is the same kind as the marble that was used to build the Parthenon in Athens, Greece.

The terrace is decorated with oversize stone urns, **ornate** lampposts, and two incredible flagpoles. The flagpoles, rarely noticed by visitors, are marvelous, fanciful concoctions of **Classical** figures from mythology and legend, good examples of the profusion of Classical detailing used throughout the library. Four winged human figures encircle each pole: one, called Navigation, holds the Argo, the boat that the ancient Greek hero Jason took on his journey to find the Golden Fleece. Another, Discovery, holds a globe; Conquest, a sword; and Civilization, a book, of course. Entwined in and around these figures are leaves, vines, and garlands of various sorts, as well as tiny **zodiac** figures. This menagerie is supported on the backs of four turtles, and the entire thing, eighty-seven feet high, is topped with an eagle. All this on a simple flagpole! You can see the extreme attention to detail, imagination, and thought that went into the design and decoration of the library.

The library is often identified by its two familiar pink marble lions that greet visitors on the main staircase. They were carved by Edward Clark Potter in 1911, the year the library opened (the ceremony was held on May 24). Later, they were named *Patience* and *Fortitude* by Mayor Fiorello La Guardia, to symbolize the two qualities most needed to survive in New York during the Great Depression. (They still serve as good reminders of these virtues.) The lions have been adopted by generations of New Yorkers and visitors, who lovingly decorate them with flowers in the spring, and holly wreaths around their necks in the winter.

The main entrance on Fifth Avenue is appropriately grand. Its twin coupled columns and the approach by a monumental flight of steps help to identify the building as a work of **Beaux Arts Classicism**. The front doors are located in three large, **arched** porticoes under an **entablature** carrying six monumental Classical statues. On either side of the entrance are symmetrical wings of strong, simple design. The twenty-two heavy **Corinthian** columns on the main facade are its most distinctive feature; they lend an air of dignity, but are not as overpowering as the twenty Corinthian columns on McKim, Mead & White's James A. Farley Post Office Building (1910–13), a designated landmark across town at West 32nd Street and Eighth Avenue.

When you enter the library through one of the porticoes, you are standing in Astor Hall, instantly surrounded by marble in a marvelously designed space. The **vaulted** ceilings are constructed entirely of white marble, and are completely self-supporting, with no posts or interior rods for support. The floor is set with geometric designs made from colored marbles. While the columns on the outside of the building are made of stone drums, that is, of cylindrical pieces of marble stacked one on top of another, like layers of a birthday cake, the columns inside are **monoliths**—single, flawless pieces of marble, with vertical veining. Carrère & Hastings were so meticulous in demanding excellent, flawless marbles that nearly 60 percent of the imported stone was rejected. It was eventually used, however, in the construction of other buildings, such as the Harvard Medical School in Cambridge, Massachusetts.

The interior of a great library requires a very specialized sort of design. Large research libraries like the New York Public Library do not circulate books—they must be read at the library. (The New York Public Library originally had a smaller lending library on the ground floor, in a room with a beautiful **cast-iron** ceiling—it is now a lecture and concert hall called the Celeste Bartos Forum.) Therefore, there has to be a comfortable place for the many people who use the library to read and study, which is called a reading room. Such libraries may have millions of books, kept on shelves that are called **stacks**. Since it would be chaotic for each reader to go into the stacks to find his or her own books, such a library must also have an efficient way to deliver books from the stacks to readers. These requirements make the insides of libraries like no other buildings in the world.

The first great free public library was the British Library, attached to the British Museum in London. Here, the famous public reading room, which opened in 1857, was arranged in a great circle under the main **dome** of the building. The reading room of the Library of Congress in Washington, D.C. (1897), was similarly arranged. The main reading room at the New York Public Library is a rectangular hall larger than either of these, its size reflecting the importance of its purpose, for in this peaceful room hundreds of people can read and study in comfort. Sitting above seven floors of book stacks, it overlooks Bryant Park and is safely removed from the street noise of the busy intersection at Fifth Avenue and 42nd Street. Oversized arched windows high on the walls allow sunlight in for reading. This room, too, has an elaborate ceiling, not supported by columns or posts but made from suspended plaster and wire, painted in gold, with intricate cherubs

and vines. The tables, chairs, and bronze reading lamps, all designed by Carrère & Hastings, became intimately familiar to generations of New Yorkers who looked upon this room as a free university, and who used the knowledge gained in it to achieve better lives. Here, historically significant events have originated. For example, Supreme Court arguments for both sides of the *Brown v. Board of Education* (1954) law case—which established the rule that separate schools for blacks and whites did not fulfill the constitutional requirement of equal treatment, and led to the desegregation of American public schools—were based on research done in this room.

Eighty-eight *miles* of bookshelves are stored within the library's original seven levels of book stacks. The entire system of book storage and retrieval, which routinely delivers any book on request within fifteen minutes to a desk centrally located in the main reading room above the stacks, was designed by engineer Bernard Richardson Green, who designed a similar system for the Library of Congress. His plans, which included **pneumatic tubes** to carry call slips from the request desk to the stacks, were so innovative they were featured on the cover of *Scientific American* in 1911. Today, the library's resources have expanded to the point where an additional eighty-eight miles of bookshelves are going to be housed in new climate-controlled stacks underneath Bryant Park.

To see more of the remarkably elaborate decorative embellishment and sculpted ornament in the library, you must visit the special-collection rooms and exhibition halls. Of course, not all books are kept in the general stacks. Rare books are singled out in various special collections; artbooks also have their own room, and so do prints. Over the years, as the main collection grew, other special collections developed their own libraries, such as the Performing Arts Library at Lincoln Center for the Performing Arts, at Broadway and 66th Street, and the Schomburg Center for Research in Black Culture, at Lenox Avenue and 135th Street. A new library of science and business is planned to open in the former B. Altman & Co. department store, a landmark at 34th Street and Fifth Avenue.

If you visit the library, you must be sure to visit some of the more spectacularly decorated rooms that have been restored, as well as the more workaday collections where great feats of research and writing have been accomplished. The Gottesman Exhibition Hall is a good place to start. When you enter this room, be sure to look up—it has a rare, beautifully carved oak ceiling. This is the place where you will find, among other things, Thomas Jefferson's handwritten copy of the Declaration of Independence, and the first typeset version of it, too; Lenox's Gutenberg Bible; and the oldest object in the library: a five-thousand-year-old "book" of sorts, a tiny clay cone completely inscribed with symbols belonging to an ancient Sumerian form of writing called cuneiform.

The DeWitt Wallace Periodicals Room, at the south end of the library, is named for the founder of *Reader's Digest* magazine, who, with his wife, Lila Acheson Wallace, was often here gathering anecdotes, quips, and quotes for their publication. The Lila Acheson Wallace Foundation gave funds for this room's restoration in 1983, preserving the gorgeous German gray marble doorways, the inlaid ebony and fruitwood tables, and the ornately carved ceiling, made of plaster stained to look like wood.

The Map Room, at the north end of the library, mirrors the periodicals room at the other end of the building. It has not yet been restored. The quality and quantity of maps kept here rival any other collection in the world. During World War II, the Allied forces (principally the United States, England, and France) used maps of Algeria, Tunisia, and Morocco from this collection to plan the invasion of French West Africa. In the Science and Technology Division, across the hall from the Map Room, scientist Edwin Land found the information he needed to develop the first Polaroid camera. Another person, Chester Carlton, developed the Xerox photocopier the same way. The Art Division is the only place in the world that has records sufficient to trace the authenticity of Vincent van Gogh's painting *Sunflowers*, which was sold at auction in 1990 for a then record-setting $45 million.

The New York Public Library is one of the five most important research libraries in the world, ranked with the Library of Congress, the Bibliothèque Nationale in Paris, the British Library in London, and the Lenin Library in Moscow (which was closed in 1991, unable to finance renovations mandated by the health department). Among its impressive collections are 300,000 Russian- and other Slavic-language books and 250,000 Oriental volumes. As a matter of fact, when the library opened in 1911, among the very first books requested was one in Russian! The library is also doing its part to preserve the events of today for the future. For example, it is gathering a unique collection of posters, pamphlets, placards, and tape recordings made during the 1989 Tiananmen Square revolt in China.

U.S. Custom House

1907

U.S. Custom
House

The remarkable rate of growth and change that has made New York City's history different from almost every other city's was fueled in the nineteenth century by trade and immigration. These days, when we travel long distances by plane or train or car, we may forget that before the Civil War, shipping was the most efficient and economical way to get people and goods from place to place. From 1789, when the United States Custom Service was first established, until 1852, nearly 80 percent—more than double all other ports combined—of the country's income from import taxes was collected at the New York Custom House, almost all on goods shipped by sea. Well into the twentieth century, New York's port was a major entry point for goods coming into this country.

The national government taxes many goods imported from foreign countries; these taxes are collected as the goods arrive and pass through "customs." If you know anyone who has traveled to another country, or have done so yourself, you may be familiar with paying "duty," or "customs." When a traveler returns to the United States, a fee is charged for things that were purchased abroad if the total of the purchases exceeds a certain amount (today, it's four hundred dollars per adult for each thirty days of travel), with a limit on the frequency of tax-exempt purchases permitted. The customs has a dual purpose: to protect United States industries from foreign competition by making the imported goods more competitive with domestic goods, and to serve as a revenue source for the country.

As you probably remember, the Revolutionary War was started as a result of the Colonies' opposition to customs placed on goods arriving in this country. Colonists were opposed to paying a tax to the British government on important commodities like tea. In 1773, a group of Bostonians dressed as Indians staged a protest against British-imposed import taxes that had raised the price of tea a considerable amount. The costumed men boarded ships from the British East India Tea Company, and dumped its cargo—tea—into Boston Harbor. This was, of course, what became known as the Boston Tea Party.

Until income taxes were enacted in 1913, the federal government depended on the cus-

tecting the young city from attack by sea, for over 150 years. The last fort was razed in 1789, when it was thought that New York City would remain the United States capital, which it had been since 1785. Optimistically, a residence for George Washington, called Government House, was built where the fort had been; this became a home for the governor of New York when the nation's capital was moved to Philadelphia in 1790. Abandoned again when the seat of state government was moved to Albany in 1797, the house became a tavern until the government took it over for its customs operations in 1799. In 1815, the ill-fated building burned to the ground.

In 1899, after the site of the new Custom House had been selected, a **design competition** was announced, and twenty of the nation's foremost architects were asked to submit proposals for the building. By November of that year, the jury selected the then relatively unknown architect Cass Gilbert. Other than his design of the state capitol building in St. Paul, Minnesota (his hometown), little of Gilbert's work was widely known. The choice was not well received by many associated with the project—particularly some of the other architects who submitted proposals—because the quiet midwestern architect, who received his training at the Massachusetts Institute of Technology, was not thought to be "established" enough for such a prestigious assignment.

Gilbert, who spent the 1880s with McKim, Mead & White, the firm that designed more of New York City's important buildings than any other, believed that public buildings should encourage "pride in the state, [be] an education to oncoming generations . . . [and] a symbol of the civilization, culture and ideals of our country."

toms taxes it collected to maintain its operations. So it was obvious that a distinguished and dependable place for the collection of all this money was needed. Two buildings that the Custom Service outgrew are still standing: Federal Hall National Memorial, at 28 Wall Street, was the Custom House from 1842 to 1862; Citibank, at 55 Wall Street, served as the Custom House from 1863 to 1899. In 1897, Treasury Secretary Lyman J. Gage allocated money for a new building on a far grander scale than the earlier ones.

A historic plot of land was chosen at the very southern point of Manhattan, the site of an earlier Custom House. The area is still called Bowling Green, because, as you might suspect, it was once used as an out-of-doors bowling alley. In 1626, Fort Amsterdam was built there, and a fort occupied the site continuously, pro-

His magnificent Custom House now stands in the shadows of, but is in no way diminished by, the **skyscrapers** that have grown around it.

While the Custom House is not tall, it is *massive*. Despite its seven-story height, the building's volume is one-quarter that of the eighty-six-story Empire State Building. A work of **Beaux Arts Classicism** (note again the use of coupled **columns**), the exterior is a fantasy of ornamentation, but under the stone facing is an up-to-date **steel** frame. The **limestone**, **granite**, and **marble** required for the construction of the Custom House cost close to $2.5 million. Mechanical equipment and interior decorations brought the costs to over $7 million, a great deal of money in those days, even for an important government building.

With this lavish budget, provided by the federal government, Cass Gilbert could create a structure that conveyed wealth and power, appropriate to the Custom Service's contribution to the United States economy. Avoiding such conventional features of public buildings as large **domes** and Classical **porticoes**, Gilbert instead chose to adorn the building with sculpture and decorative architectural flourishes. This rich ornamentation reflects the prevailing taste in public buildings of the time. This is a good building to use to practice identifying the elements of Classical architecture.

Since the U.S. Custom House was a focal point for worldwide overseas trade, it was appropriate to use maritime **motifs**, like dolphins, shells, masts, anchors, and waves, to decorate the walls, in addition to the more traditional Classical motifs and **moldings**. Above the second-floor windows, eight **keystone** sculptures embody different ethnic groups, selected according to ideas that were current around the turn of the century: Caucasian, Hindu, Latin, Celtic, Mongolian, Eskimo, Slav, and African. On the **frieze** above each **capital** is a stone carving of the head of Mercury, the god of commerce in Roman mythology, symbolizing both commerce and antiquity.

The most outstanding sculptural works on the exterior of the U.S. Custom House are the immense white limestone figures seated on pedestals at the ground-floor level at the front entrance. The American sculptor Daniel Chester French, who was responsible for the enormous seated sculpture of Abraham Lincoln at the Lincoln Memorial in Washington, D.C., was commissioned by Cass Gilbert to create the figures, called "The Continents." Each figure represents one of four continents—

Arch over the main entrance

North America, Europe, Asia, and Africa.

Gilbert requested that each of the figures be in a seated position, in order to convey a sense of composure and gravity. At the building's attic level, one is treated to twelve more sculpted figures. These represent the most prosperous nations in history, beginning with the civilizations of Greece and Rome, and ending with France and Great Britain. The sculptures form a **narrative**, reading from left to right, of the growth of maritime commerce through the ages. Cass Gilbert underscored the leadership of the United States as the world's major commercial power by placing symbols of the nation in places of prominence throughout the building. Centered above the **facade** is an enormous **cartouche**, carved by the Austrian sculptor Karl Bitter, that presents the national seal of the United States suspended between two figures symbolizing peace and unity, with the American eagle positioned above and a bound bundle of reeds, the symbol of strength in unity, below. The **lintel** over the entrance weighs thirty tons, and was quarried on Hurricane Island off the coast of Maine. It was transported to New York on a three-masted schooner.

The interior of the Custom House continues the richness of materials and decoration established by the exterior. The main entrance, through a large, **arched** doorway, leads to a magnificent two-story hall that is covered in sixteen different types of marble from all over the world. Switzerland, Italy, Alaska, Georgia, Vermont, and many other places are represented by the various colors, patterns, and textures of elegant stone. The main hall is divided into three central **bays**, separated by arches. Smaller bays flanking the hall contain matching spiral staircases that circle all the way to the top floor. The **vaulted** ceilings of the bays were painted with **allegorical murals** by the artist Elmer E. Garnsey.

This hall bisects the main floor of the building, separating the elaborate front offices from the **rotunda** and the back offices, where the day-to-day work of collecting customs and counting, as accounting was once called, was carried out. The doorways and arches have carvings of ship bows and sea creatures.

From the main hall, the visitor passes through a **vestibule** with an open arch to enter the rotunda, a magnificent space that measures 135 feet by 85 feet and soars 48 feet high. The rotunda's construction is noteworthy because the great dome holds up a 140-ton skylight, but it does so with no visible means of support. Nor does it rely on a keystone system for bracing, like many arched or vaulted structures. Designed by the Spanish engineer and artist Rafael Guastavino, the elliptical rotunda is constructed of 140 tons of tiles and plaster. The original skylight was tarred over during World War II, when buildings were required to cloak all windows under blackout regulations to avoid becoming targets in potential enemy attacks, but it has since been replaced.

Gilbert had originally intended there to be murals in the rotunda, but the appropriation for the building's construction was not large enough to pay an artist. In 1937, during the Great Depression, the Treasury Relief Art Project, a program to assist artists established by the Treasury Department, commissioned painter Reginald Marsh to decorate the vaulting in the rotunda. Marsh, an artist known for his realistic—often gritty—depictions of life in the city, painted a series of **frescoes** that are a narrative of New York's harbor. Illustrating this 2,300-square-foot "canvas" posed an unusual challenge to Marsh. Since his paintings would be viewed from below, and because of the curve of the space, it became necessary for him to adjust his drawings so they would not look distorted. The eight large paintings show a ship journeying through New York Harbor. The ship meets up with the Coast Guard, passes the Statue of Liberty, and even stops for a press interview with the actress Greta Garbo before being escorted to a pier by tugboats, where its cargo is unloaded. Eight smaller panels, also painted by Marsh, show early American explorers.

In the northwest corner of the Custom House is the extravagant office originally built for the treasury secretary of the United States. Paneled from floor to ceiling in oak by Tiffany Studios, the office is now called the Commissioner's Office. Above the marble fireplace is this inscription: "On this site Fort Amsterdam was erected in 1626. Government House was built in 1790 for President Washington. Here Geo. Clinton and John Jay lived. Used as Custom House from 1799 to 1815." The room is circled by a gilded frieze, or band, where the walls meet the ceiling, embellished with nautical figures. The ceiling is decorated with **coffers** in a pattern of recessed octagonal panels, and is gilded with dark, gold-colored aluminum leaf. The Commissioner's Office also has paintings by Elmer E. Garnsey, which show images of early Dutch and English settlers that relate to commerce. Next door, the Manager's Office offers a stark contrast to the opulence of the neighboring Commissioner's Office. It has plain white plaster walls with a simple **Ionic cornice**.

The Cashier's Office, where the public came to make payments, is in the northeast corner of the building. The room is divided by a long white marble counter topped by a bronze screen. The main wall of the public's half of the room is marble, while the area behind the screen, where cashiers worked, has plaster walls. The doorway moldings are decorated with more carved nautical figures, and the ceiling is an elaborate plaster replica of a gilded **Renaissance** boxed-beam design.

In 1973, the United States Customs Service moved its operations to the World Trade Center, and the Custom House was left with an uncertain future. Operated now by the United States General Services Administration, the Custom House—if all continues according to plan—will soon house the George Gustav Heye Center, an exhibition site for the new National Museum of the American Indian. This will permit the old Museum of the American Indian, which is moving its collections from Audubon Terrace at 155th Street and Broadway to Washington, D.C., where it will become a part of the Smithsonian Institution, to maintain a continuing presence in New York City. The design of the new museum calls for restoring the rotunda; renovating the rest of the main floor for a children's orientation room, museum shop, and offices; and creating a permanent gallery on the second floor for exhibitions. The third floor and above are used for federal offices, including bankruptcy court.

The U.S. Custom House's decorations, sculptures, and interior murals tell tales of shipping and trade, and of the mighty sea that made the exchange of goods possible. This substantial building is the symbol of a nation that envisioned itself as the world's leader in commerce and industry.

Grand Central
Terminal

1913

In 1850, New York City was by far the largest city in the United States, followed by Baltimore, Boston, and Philadelphia—all port cities on the Eastern seaboard. Fifty years later, the nation's second-largest city was Chicago, deep inside North America. All across America in those fifty years, people were leaving the established centers of population for new places. And what made this vast movement of people possible was the railroad.

In 1850, there was no railroad service between New York City and the small town of Chicago, and the trip was not one to be taken lightly. Fifty years later—fifty-two to be exact—the new Twentieth Century Limited covered the route in twenty hours. By 1932, you could get on the train in Chicago and be in New York City sixteen and a half hours later, traveling on a train that entered the metropolis unobtrusively by underground tracks, and disembark in a magnificent station in the heart of the city, where you could get a subway, bus, or car to your ultimate destination. If you were simply a **commuter**, you could travel to and from work by the same means. What made all of this possible was Grand Central Terminal, one of the great modern achievements of transportation architecture and engineering.

The concept of a central station, where all tracks would meet, was the idea of a man named Cornelius Vanderbilt. As did many before the advent of the railroad, Vanderbilt had once believed that water transportation was the most efficient way to travel. He was so involved with his ships, and the shipping industry, that he was nicknamed Commodore. (A commodore was a naval officer with the rank just above captain and below rear admiral.) Born to a modest farming family on Staten Island in 1794, Cornelius Vanderbilt died in 1877 at the age of eighty-two, leaving an estate worth more than $100 million. He began his business at sixteen, with a small sailing boat ferrying people between Staten Island and Manhattan. During the next several decades, the Commodore continued to purchase ferry and steamship lines until he managed to control the major shipping companies in the Northeast. It was only after he turned sixty that Vanderbilt began to realize the possibilities of

Grand Central

Terminal

115

train travel, and by then he had made enough money to buy entire railroad lines!

Three railroads formed the nucleus of his empire—the New York and Harlem Railroad, the Hudson River Railroad, and the New York Central. The first two of these companies connected New York City (the island of Manhattan) with Westchester and points north. The Central, as it was called, provided access from Albany to the west.

Cornelius Vanderbilt had little trouble gaining control of the New York and Harlem Railroad in 1862 and the Hudson River Railroad a year later. He simply went and bought **stocks** in the individual companies until stockholders had no choice but to give him control. (Stockholders are generally thought to cede control to the person, or the representative of the group, that owns the most, or a majority, of a company's stock. Frequently, whoever owns more than 50 percent of a company's stock tries to gain, or retain, control.)

He had some difficulty, however, gaining control of the Central, and he was waging constant war with it over how to divide the income from fares and freight and how to apportion the costs of maintaining track. So he developed a strategy to humble the line. The New York Central Railroad carried passengers and freight from Buffalo and points west to Albany. In order to get to New York City, passengers and freight would take either Hudson River steamboats or Vanderbilt's Hudson River Railroad, which was accessible via a bridge across the Hudson at Albany that opened in 1866. When the river was frozen in the winter, the Central had no choice but to use Vanderbilt's trains to take its passengers and freight to New York City. On January 14, 1867, Vanderbilt in-

formed the New York Central Railroad that he would refuse to accept transfers from its trains to his Hudson River Railroad. Imagine what it was like for passengers who, in the depth of winter and weighted down with luggage, had to cross the long windy bridge on foot! Newspapers protested, and the New York State Legislature began an investigation of Vanderbilt, but soon the Central acceded to all of Vanderbilt's demands. In the meanwhile, the value of stock in the New York Central Railroad plummeted, and Vanderbilt began to purchase large blocks of stock at the low price. In the end, Vanderbilt owned enough stock in the New York Central Railroad that the stockholders had no choice but to offer him control of the company. Soon after, Vanderbilt bought the Lake Shore and Michigan Southern Railroad. When his son William added the Michigan Central in 1878, one year after the Commodore's death, the Vanderbilts had a direct route to Chicago and controlled a major share of both long-distance and commuter transportation in New York City.

Vanderbilt's consolidated lines required a central train station. Where this train station would be built was essentially influenced by a law that went into effect in 1857. Until the 1940s most trains in the United States were run by steam. Steam engines were often a great nuisance and hazard to the people who lived and worked in areas close to the tracks. They were noisy and dirty, and occasionally threw off sparks that started fires. In 1857, the New York City Council had heard so many complaints that it banned steam engines south of 42nd Street in Manhattan, where most people worked and lived. The new rule meant that steam engines were permitted only north of

42nd Street.

Trains then had to be uncoupled from their engines at the edge of the city and hauled by horse to the depot at East 26th Street. Vanderbilt decided that it would be more efficient if his train station were located above 42nd Street, so that he would not have to go through the difficulty of uncoupling his trains and towing them downtown. In preparation for his plan, Vanderbilt bought a tract of land between Lexington Avenue and Madison Avenue from 42nd to 48th Street.

Shortly thereafter, in May of 1869, the state of New York gave Vanderbilt permission to build his train station, which he planned to call Grand Central, at 42nd Street and Park Avenue. The first stone of the new train station was laid in September of 1869. The area, which is now called midtown, was barely inhabited at that time. Most of the city's activities were centered in the downtown area, below 42nd Street. In fact, many people laughed at the name Vanderbilt decided to give to the new station, since it was hardly central to New York City! But Vanderbilt was shrewd. He recognized that New York City's rapidly growing population, just under a million by 1869, would increasingly force people to live and work farther uptown.

Construction was completed in 1871. Grand Central Depot was built in two years, at a cost of three million dollars. The work was carried out under the direction of the Commodore and his son William. It was the first American train station that could even begin to compare to the beautiful railway stations of Europe, such as the second Paddington Station (1852–54) in London, the Gare de l'Est (1847–52), and the **renovated** Gare du Nord (1861–65) in Paris.

New York's Grand Central Depot, designed by John B. Snook, was, like most big city stations, of the **head-house** type, meaning that trains could either back in or back out of the main building but could not run through the station. The depot building was constructed so that there was a main train shed and three separate waiting rooms, one for each of the three train lines (in addition to Vanderbilt's New York and Harlem Railroad and the consolidated New York Central and Hudson Railroad, the New York and New Haven leased space in the station). Railroad offices were located on the upper floors.

The station was famous for its great train shed, the largest interior space in North America at that time and a tourist attraction in its own right. Designed by R. G. Hatfield and Joseph Duclos, the shed was two hundred feet wide and six hundred feet long, and the roof, which rose to one hundred feet, was supported by thirty semicircular-shaped **trusses** manufactured by Daniel D. Badger's Architectural Iron Works. Three **monitors** brought light to the room during the day; at night the room was lit by twelve large gas-fired chandeliers. The station had twelve tracks and five platforms.

It took only a short time before many problems with the **layout** of the new train station became obvious. Arriving passengers could not go directly into the distant waiting rooms but had to walk around the tracks. The baggage room was also very inconvenient: it was located in the train shed, and anyone who wanted to pick up baggage had to have a ticket. By 1872, there were 130 trains each day entering or leaving the station. It was so hectic and noisy that no locomotive bells or whistles could be sounded unless there was an emergency. Had the bells been used, the noise would have been constant.

By 1898, it became apparent that the depot had to be renovated. New York architect Bradford L. Gilbert, who had designed the Illinois Central Station in Chicago, was hired to design a new train shed with seven more tracks to accommodate the by now more than five hundred trains that passed through the station daily. The depot building was enlarged and three more floors were built. Two years later a single waiting room replaced the three previous ones and a new waiting room was put in the basement to accommodate the influx of immigrants who were arriving in New York from all over the world. By the time the renovations were completed, the area around Grand Central had become more fashionable. In 1897, the popular dining-and-dancing club Sherry's opened on the southeast corner of Fifth Avenue and 44th Street; Delmonico's, a fashionable restaurant, was on the northeast side of the street. Many men's clubs also sprouted in the neighborhood.

The problems persisted. From the first opening of the train station, the traffic had been heavy. Smoke and steam from locomotives filled the two miles of tunnel tracks leading to the station, making it virtually impossible for conductors to read the signals. Inevitably, a major accident made the city of New York reconsider its policy on steam engines. On January 8, 1902, an inbound New York Central train, whose engineer had been unable to see a red light at 54th Street, crashed into the rear of a New Haven train. Fifteen people died in the accident. The public, outraged by the smoke problems and the accidents, of which this was only the worst, complained bitterly to the city government. In July 1908, the New York State Legislature banned all steam-operated trains south of the Harlem River. As it turned out, New York Central Railroad vice president William J. Wilgus had been investigating the possibility of powering trains with electricity before the new rule came into effect.

By 1900, electrically powered trains were being used all over the world. In America, the first electric-powered streetcar had been used in 1885 in Richmond, Virginia, and General Electric had been manufacturing electric locomotives since 1895. On October 23, 1899, the first electric trolley cars appeared in New York City, on the Third Avenue Surface Line.

Wilgus's plan was to have the trains run through tunnels under Park Avenue on a single level until they reached 50th Street, where the tracks would divide and enter the station on two levels. With the tracks and train yards underground, it would be possible, Wilgus argued, to build offices, apartment buildings, and shops in the seventeen-block area above the tunnels. This was a new idea, since nothing could be built over the tunnels when the trains had been steam powered. When trains were run by steam, it was necessary to have open spaces above the tunnels to allow the steam to clear. Without steam, the area on top of the tunnels could be developed. In other words, whoever owned the land occupied by the tunnels could take advantage of their **"air rights."** (Air rights refer to the so-called right to use the air space over preexisting structures. Generally, the ownership of land includes the right to use the surface, the ground below, and the air above. Many real-estate owners build not only on the surface, but also over earlier construction. For example, if you owned an office build-

Sculpture of Mercury, Hercules, and Minerva crowning the main facade

GRAND CENTRAL
TERMINAL

ing, you *may* have the right to build on top of it—perhaps more stories, or even a tower, because you own the air *above* the building.)

Many architectural firms submitted **plans** to carry out Wilgus's ideas. Two firms, Reed & Stem of St. Paul, Minnesota, and Warren & Wetmore of New York City, were ultimately chosen to design and orchestrate the construction of the new depot. Some people claimed that nepotism, or favoritism, was involved in the final choice of a design team. Charles Reed, a named partner in the architectural firm of Reed & Stem, happened to be Wilgus's brother-in-law. Whitney Warren, of Warren & Wetmore, was a cousin of the old Commodore's grandson, William K. Vanderbilt, who was the chairman of the board of the New York Central and Hudson River Railroad. Regardless of the gossip, both firms had established reputations for excellent work. Warren & Wetmore had

won a **design competition** in 1899 for a new clubhouse for the New York Yacht Club, a designated landmark at 37 West 44th Street. The Reed & Stem firm had previously designed more than five terminals, including the New York Central and Hudson River's new station at Troy, New York. The responsibilities for the new train station were divided as follows: Reed & Stem were assigned the engineering part of the project; Warren & Wetmore were in charge of the design of the building.

The new Grand Central Terminal, as it was called, took nearly ten years to construct, from June, 1903, to February, 1913. Most people are rightly impressed with the size of the building. Grand Central Terminal was meant to be not only a train station; it was also designed to be a symbol of the advances in train travel.

The **facade** of the building reinforces the impression that this building is of great importance. Whitney Warren said that the facade was designed to appear as if it were a gate to one of the great ancient walled cities. Six pairs of **Doric columns**—note again the characteristic coupled columns of beaux arts architecture—stand between the three huge **arched** windows. Crowning the main facade is a statue of three **mythological** gods surrounding a thirteen-foot clock. Mercury, the god of commerce, stands on top of the clock. On one side lies Hercules, symbolic of morality; on the other, Minerva, the goddess of creative energy. Carved by the French sculptor Jules-Alexis Coutan from Bedford **limestone**, the three gods are a monument to the hard work and creativity of those who contributed to the development of train travel. The sculpture weighs about fifteen hundred tons; it is sixty feet wide and fifty feet high!

The materials used on the exterior of the building are Stony Creek **granite** and Bedford limestone. The walls inside the station are made to look like stone but are actually made of **terra-cotta**. All the trim and **wainscoting** are Bottocino **marble**, and the floors are paved with Tennessee marble. Approximately $2 million worth of bronze was used for screens, window frames, railings, and the train gates.

In addition to making the station appear grand, the architects also intended to make the station more efficient for both trains and travelers. One of their first projects was to make it easier for more trains to go in and out of the station. By the time the rebuilding was in full swing there were more than eleven hundred trains passing through Grand Central each day. As you may remember, the original station was designed so that trains could only back in or out of the station. Additional land was there-

fore purchased for a two-level loop that would make it possible for trains to circle around underground and leave the station without backing up.

Another goal of the renovation was to make it easier for travelers to get information and experience a pleasant wait for their trains. The great main **concourse**—275 feet long by 120 feet wide—accomplished this goal. This room housed all the important functions of a train station, such as the ticket windows, baggage rooms, and information booth. By day, light streamed through three great arched windows that were almost 60 feet high. Five **clerestory lunettes** high up in the 125-foot **vault** provided additional light. At night, large bronze chandeliers lit the vast space. To give the room a celestial feel, Warren & Wetmore commissioned a **mural** of a Mediterranean sky for the ceiling. The design, taken by Warren from a painting by Paul Helleu, shows a starry sky at night with the constellations of the **zodiac**. (Today, the mural is dim and the chandeliers are gone.)

Off the main concourse is a waiting room also of imposing dimensions—65 feet by 205 feet—that has lost its elegance and charm. At opposite ends of the room there were once separate men's and women's waiting rooms and restrooms. The women's waiting room, located at the east end, had a hair salon and a shoeshine shop. In the men's waiting room, at the west end, there were a barbershop, baths, dressing rooms, and a smoking room.

A separate concourse with low ceilings was designed on the lower level of the terminal, directly below the main concourse, with ticket windows, baggage rooms, and information booth. Also on the lower level, and worth a detour to look at, is the famous Oyster Bar, with a vaulted ceiling of terra-cotta tiles and plaster by Rafael Guastavino, similar in technique to his **rotunda** in the U.S. Custom House (see pages 108–13).

The main goal of Grand Central's design was for travelers to have easier access to trains and exits. The key to its success was the sloping ramps that connect the various exits and the lower and upper levels of the station, and which, in contrast to stairs, permit large crowds to circulate easily. Despite the station's great size, the architects successfully arranged it so that there were many direct routes between the street and the tracks to accommodate the more than twenty million passengers who would use it the year it opened.

After Grand Central Terminal was completed, at a cost of about $72 million, the area between East 42nd Street and East 52nd Street became one of the most fashionable in New York City, and Park Avenue, particularly, was lined with luxurious apartment buildings and hotels. By the late 1920s almost all of the air rights above the tunnels had been sold and the land developed. Between 1904 and 1920 the value of land in that area increased at a rate of almost 250 percent. Today this area is still considered very desirable, and real estate there is expensive.

For many people, Grand Central is one of the most distinguished and familiar landmarks in New York City. The circular information booth on the main concourse, with its huge four-faced golden clock, became a familiar meeting place. The phrase "like Grand Central Station" is still widely used to describe a place that is bustling and crowded.

In 1946, Grand Central experienced its most profitable and busy year. Since then, airplane and automobile travel have by and large replaced train travel, and the station has lost money and prestige. While commuters continue to use trains to travel to work, trains are no longer used for intercity travel with the same frequency as they were in the 1940s. With increased, and swifter, choices of transportation, people do not wish to spend as much money on train travel; in turn, train stations do not make as much money as they did when trains were the main form of transportation. In 1954, the railroad lost about $25 million on the operation of the station. It became difficult to maintain the huge building.

The lack of financial security led Grand Central Terminal into a period of instability. The air rights above the station and the area around the station had

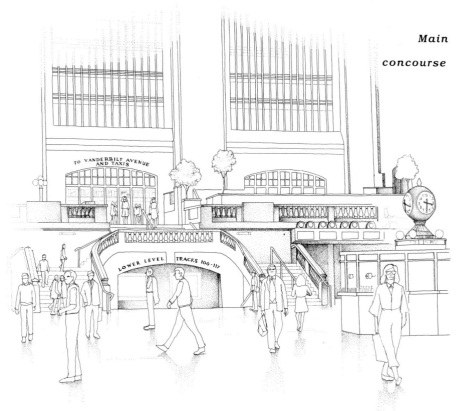

Main concourse

Mercury

developers was given permission to construct a building on top of the north end of the station. The fifty-nine-story building was originally to be called Grand Central City, but was finally named the Pan Am Building, after the main tenant. After the Pan Am Building was completed, proposals continued to be presented. One proposal suggested that the waiting room off the main concourse be divided into four fifteen-foot stories, with the upper story to be made into a bowling alley! This proposal revealed an absolute lack of concern for the dignity and spirit of the station. It is difficult to believe that the proposers could have envisioned a bowling alley as being appropriate to the elegance Warren & Wetmore had intended when they designed the station. Immediately following the bowling alley proposal, a public hearing with eighty witnesses was held before the New York City Landmarks Preservation Commission. As you may recall from the opening chapter of this book, the Landmarks Preservation Commission is responsible for designating a building a landmark, and making sure that landmarks are not destroyed or damaged or changed in any inappropriate way. All changes to the exterior of designated landmarks are required by law to be reviewed by the commission. On August 2, 1967, the commission designated Grand Central Terminal a landmark.

Still the station was confronted with proposals for development. In 1968, less than five years after the Pan Am Building opened, and less than one year after the station was designated a landmark, a British real-estate developer, Morris Saady, who had leased the air rights above the terminal, came up with a plan to construct a tower on top of the station. The tower would be designed by the famous modern

become very valuable. Many businesses wished to have offices around the terminal. The prestige of having an office in a fashionable neighborhood, in addition to the convenience of proximity to the station, made development over the station seem highly desirable. The station was barraged with proposals for developments. These proposals, however, created an upheaval. There were, of course, at least two sides to the argument. Those who were in favor of development recognized that the terminal was in desperate need of money, for both maintenance and operating costs. Those in opposition to such proposals were concerned that a new building could possibly destroy or detract from the design the station's architects had worked so hard to create.

In the early 1960s, a group of real-estate

architect Marcel Breuer, and the proposal included the promise that the station would be restored to its original elegance. The application for permission to build the tower was presented to the Landmarks Preservation Commission.

On September 20, 1968, after four days of hearings, the commission denied the application for the tower. The commission thought that the new tower would not enhance the exterior of Grand Central Terminal. The commission was also concerned that the tower would ruin the dramatic view of the terminal from Park Avenue South.

In April of the following year, a new design was presented to the commission. This application was also denied. Frustrated with their desire to develop the property by building a tower on top of the station, Penn Central (the owners of the station) brought suit against the New York City Landmarks Preservation Commission in New York State court. Penn Central claimed that the Landmarks Law was unconstitutional because it unreasonably restricted their right to use the property. Essentially, Penn Central claimed that as the owner of a landmark, they could not make a profit from their property or investment. They also argued that landmark buildings were bearing burdens and restrictions not imposed on other landowners, and that this was discriminatory. The trial court agreed with Penn Central and declared the law unconstitutional. The court ordered that the landmarks law could not be used to stop the construction of the tower, and ordered that the designation and the commission's denial of the permit to build be struck down. The Landmarks Preservation Commission appealed the trial court's decision, and asked the New York State Appellate Division to review the issues. The appeals court agreed with the commission and reversed the lower court's decision, finding that the landmarks law was constitutional, and that the designation of the terminal should stand. Penn Central refused to accept the decision. Another appeal by Penn Central to the New York Court of Appeals, the state's highest court, was also unsuccessful; the landmarks law was constitutional in their eyes as well. Penn Central then decided to bring the issue to the United States Supreme Court for a final review. In October, 1978, more than ten years after the commission had denied the real-estate developer's original plan, the United States Supreme Court, the highest court in the United States, upheld the New York Court of Appeal's decision that the New York City landmarks law was constitutional and that the city could deny the tower. Justice William Brennan stated in his written opinion that sometimes restrictions on development are necessary to promote and protect landmarks.

The Supreme Court's decision saved Grand Central Terminal from significant alteration. The decision tested the New York City landmarks law, and said that a land use law was a proper way to preserve the quality of life in the city, and maintain the culture and spirit of New York. The decision empowers the New York City Landmarks Preservation Commission to continue to designate buildings as landmarks and preserve their character by monitoring changes to these buildings. And, most important, it ensures that future generations will have the opportunity to see firsthand, not only read about, the architectural heritage and spirit of New York past.

Chrysler
Building

124

Chrysler Building

1928–1930

The Chrysler Building, 405 Lexington Avenue, is the first **skyscraper** that you will encounter in this book. In some parts of our country, there are towns and villages where all of the buildings, even those built today, are still more like the Bowne House than the Chrysler Building in scale (and even in their design). What makes New York, and especially Manhattan, where most of New York's skyscrapers have been built, so different?

By the 1920s, land in Manhattan had become very valuable. Many builders believed that the most efficient way to provide more work space and living space where land was very expensive was to build tall buildings (the technological breakthroughs that made this possible are described in the last chapter of this book, pages 142–50) and make them as desirable as possible to renters or buyers. Simply stated, these are the forces that created some of New York's best-loved buildings, among them the one that is for many people the most expressive of the spirit of the modern city: the Chrysler Building. This lively building has real metal hubcaps, and a **frieze** of cars made of white and gray bricks, on its **facade**. In 1930, when it was completed, it was the tallest building in New York, and the **spire** on top is still one of the most striking and sharpest peaks in the city's skyline.

After the completion of the new Grand Central Terminal in 1913, midtown Manhattan became one of the most intensively developed areas in the world. The rapid pace of building was interrupted somewhat by World War I, but then picked up in the prosperous 1920s, when new and bigger office buildings were needed for a larger work force. Among the men who competed for the rights to build on this valuable real estate were some of America's most imaginative and aggressive entrepreneurs.

The Chrysler Building was built by Walter P. Chrysler, founder of the Chrysler Corporation, the automobile manufacturer that is still a major producer of cars today. Like Andrew Carnegie, Walter Chrysler was a self-made man. He started his career as a railroad worker and then joined the Buick Motor Company, working in its automobile factory. Chrysler was an innovator. He invented new, more efficient processes for the automobile plant and, as a result, rose quickly through the ranks of the company's management.

By 1924, Chrysler had become president of the Maxwell Motor Company. There, he introduced a new car with four-wheel hydraulic brakes and a high-compression motor that he named—not surprisingly—the Chrysler. This began the well-known line of cars that are still produced today. (Many automobiles have been named after the men who produced them. Ford, Dodge, and Oldsmobile cars were all named for men who, along with Chrysler, were pioneers in the automobile industry.)

Chrysler's new car was a great success. In the first year of production, sales were over fifty million dollars, and, as a result, Walter Chrysler was able to buy the Maxwell Motor Company, which he renamed the Chrysler Corporation. In 1927, he also bought the Dodge Brothers Company, making Chrysler one of the largest automobile manufacturers in the country, along with Ford and General Motors.

Walter Chrysler was skilled at using **technology** to his advantage, not only to produce better products, but also as a way to convince people to buy his products. Technology is the art of using mechanical and scientific knowledge in a specific way to produce something. It is an art because it requires creative thought to figure out how to accomplish something new or make something work better or differently. Chrysler thought that since people associated machines with a better way of life, they would be attracted to products and symbols that reminded them of machines. One example of this was to be the Chrysler Building itself, whose styling is almost completely given over to images of machines. Sometimes his thinking was too advanced for the public, as with his Chrysler Airflow automobile of 1934. This, the most fully **streamlined** automobile that had yet been produced, was called "the most beautiful product of the machine age" by the magazine *Scientific American,* but it failed in the marketplace because people simply couldn't get used to its "modern" appearance.

By 1928, Chrysler was one of the wealthiest men in the automobile industry, and he had become interested in investing in New York City real estate. He decided on a building site on Lexington Avenue between 42nd and 43rd streets in midtown Manhattan that had previously been leased by William H. Reynolds, a former New York state senator and a **real-estate developer** and promoter, from the Cooper Union for the Advancement of Science and Art. (Cooper Union, a highly regarded tuition-free college for engineering, architecture, and the fine arts, was founded in 1859 by the inventor Peter Cooper, who built one of the first steam locomotives. The school is still in operation today, in its original building, a designated landmark on Cooper Square between Astor Place and East 7th Street, in an area now referred to as the East Village.)

Reynolds's original **plan** for a building on the site had been very grand. It was designed by William Van Alen, an architect who had trained at Pratt Institute in Brooklyn and at the Ecole des Beaux-Arts in Paris. While he was in Paris, Van Alen had discovered **Art Deco**, a popular style of contemporary French architecture and design. Reynolds and Van Alen worked together to plan a skyscraper, influenced by Art Deco, that would be sixty-seven stories high and topped with a glass **dome**, which, when it was lighted from inside, would sparkle like "a jeweled sphere."

But before construction began, Reynolds sold the land rights to Walter Chrysler. Reynolds saw a good opportunity to make a profit by selling to Chrysler—who wanted to build in a prime location. (Chrysler was investing his own money, not corporate funds, because he wanted to leave his two grown sons a building for which they could be personally responsible.) With the land, Chrysler also bought the rights to the building design that Reynolds and Van Alen had created. But Chrysler wanted to

Spire

make some changes. He asked Van Alen to substitute a pointed tower topped by a sharp spire for the dome, and to make the building about ten stories taller.

In the 1920s, the same thinking that went into creating new designs for cars went into designing buildings. People were excited about things that looked "modern" and were less attached to traditional design. The tall skyscrapers, many in the Art Deco style, that were beginning to appear on the New York skyline were monuments to the "machine age"—the new age of industry and technology.

Art Deco is a term used to describe a style of decoration used for both the interior and exterior decoration of buildings, and also for the design of many other objects, both useful and decorative, such as appliances, clothing, posters, and advertisements. The style was introduced in 1925 at a Paris design fair called the Exposition des Arts Décoratifs (Exposition of Decorative Arts)—from which it derives its name—and was almost immediately popular. It is so similar to the kind of streamlined, modern design we associate with the late 1920s and 1930s in America that some people simply call it *moderne* ("modern" with a slight nod to the French). More than one historian is content to call Van Alen's design for the Chrysler Building "automobile style," and leave it at that.

Unlike the **International Style** of modern architecture, which we will encounter when we look at Lever House and the Seagram Building (see pages 146–50), Art Deco is essentially a *decorative* style that utilizes ornamental forms, much as **Beaux Arts Classicism** does. However, the forms and **motifs** used in Art Deco design are not derived from historical styles of the past, but from modern life, and the

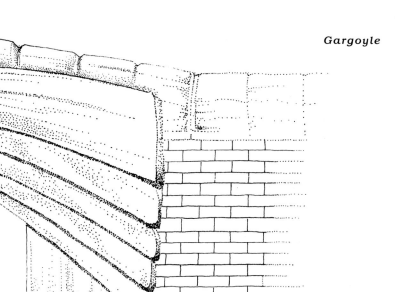

materials are decidedly new as well.

Characteristic Art Deco motifs include not only natural forms, such as plants, flowers, birds, animals, human figures, lightning bolts, clouds, suns, and stars—which had all been used as decorative elements up until that time—but also machines and other industrial objects that had become part of daily life, such as automobiles, airplanes, ocean liners, and locomotives. They also included forms that were just geometric shapes, rather than representations of identifiable objects. Such shapes strung together formed patterns, like zigzags and chevrons, that reminded people of the speedy rhythms of modern life.

Art Deco designers and architects also introduced new materials. Many older buildings in New York were decorated with carved stone or **terra-cotta**. Art Deco buildings were decorated with glass, **stainless steel**, aluminum, and even plastic. New technology made it possible to produce plastic and glass that were stronger and could be molded and shaped, and these materials opened up possibilities for architects to create dazzling new designs.

All seventy-seven stories of the Chrysler Building are a magnificent example of dramatic, elegant Art Deco design, from the bottom to the top. The building narrows from its broad base by the use of **setbacks** (where the building is literally "set back," or narrowed) at certain floors, which accounts for its graceful (and futuristic) tapering profile. The setbacks were required by New York City's 1916 **zoning** ordinance, which stated that the profile of a building had to lie within a given angle drawn from the center of the street up to a specified distance from the property line. When it was finally far back enough, the building could continue straight up as high as the builder wanted. When setbacks went out of style, builders simply began behind the permissible distance from the property line for construction without setbacks, as in Lever House and the Seagram Building (see pages 146–50). The law was not substantially altered until 1961.

On the Chrysler Building there are four setbacks below the thirty-first floor. On the walls of the building at that floor there is a frieze of automobiles made of gray and white bricks. In the centers of the wheels, there are real chrome hubcaps attached to the wall. The line of cars stretches all around the building, and at each of the four corners there is a **buttress** (a section of the wall that provides support for the building above it). On top of each buttress is a giant-sized Nirosta steel eagle, reminiscent of the image on a Chrysler radiator cap. (Nirosta steel is a rust-resistant, chromium-nickel steel from Germany that was used for the first time in the United States in the Chrysler Building.)

Above the thirty-first floor the tower of the building begins, and at the fifty-ninth floor the spire begins. At the fifty-ninth floor, there are eight Nirosta steel gargoyles. Traditional gargoyles are waterspouts in the form of grotesque figures, often carved of stone, that were used to carry water from the roof's drainpipes away from the walls of the buildings. The gargoyles on the Chrysler Building, however, are not really grotesque; they are eagles with pointy beaks. These gargoyles also are not waterspouts, only decoration, and they serve as symbols of Chrysler's automotive empire.

The spire is also made of Nirosta steel. It has six tiers of metal **arches** with triangular windows set into the arches. Each tier looks like the points of a crown, or like a sunburst with rays pointing out in many directions. The triangular window arrangement creates another geometric pattern that is typical of Art Deco style. The spire, when lit from inside at night, is one of the most magnificent sights on the New York skyline.

Topping the entire building is the **finial**, which is a sharp, pointed steel needle. This needle was William Van Alen's key to winning the race to build the tallest building in New York. At the same time that Van Alen was building the Chrysler Building, one of his for-

mer architectural partners, H. Craig Severance, was building the Bank of the Manhattan Company downtown at 40 Wall Street. Because Van Alen's original design (which he did for Reynolds) was for a 925-foot building, Severance thought he could outdo him by adding a flagpole to his bank building, making it 927 feet. But Van Alen surprised Severance, and everyone else in New York. He had the finial made in five pieces, which were secretly delivered to the construction site. One night in November, 1929, it was assembled and then hoisted into position through a fire tower in the center of the spire and riveted in place. The whole operation took about ninety minutes, and the audacity of the feat captured the popular imagination.

The finial made the building a total of 1,046 feet tall, which was even taller than the 1,024½-

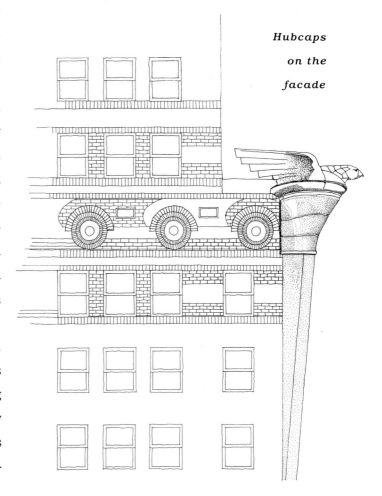

Hubcaps on the facade

foot Eiffel Tower in Paris. But the Chrysler Building was not the champion for long: the next year, in 1931, the 1,250-foot Empire State Building at 350 Fifth Avenue was completed. The desire to build the tallest building in the world is characteristic of twentieth-century architecture. Sometimes the motive has more to do with the need for recognition, for publicity, than with good building sense, but there is also a strong feeling of visionary idealism in constructing very tall buildings. The great American architect Frank Lloyd Wright once imagined a mile-high building (528 stories!) that would be surrounded by gardens and lawns. The tallest building in the world today is the 1974 Sears Tower in Chicago, at 1,454 feet still far short of Wright's imagined building.

The main entrances to the Chrysler Building, on 42nd Street and on Lexington Avenue, are large archways three stories high and out-

lined in polished black **granite**. These resemble proscenium arches. The proscenium—a word that means before (*pro*) the scenery (*scenium*)—is the part of a theater stage between the audience and the scenery. Entering the Chrysler Building is like walking under the arch of a stage, and into the scene—how dramatic! The lobby of the building is a spectacular triangular space. The walls are covered with rust-colored polished **marble**. The marble floor has a chevron pattern that directs the visitor from the entrances to the banks of elevators. Light comes into the lobby from the windows over the doorways, and there are also **cove lighting** and **sconces** along the walls, above the elevator banks, and on the **piers** in the middle of the room, which create a dramatic effect. On the ceiling there is a **mural** that brings all of the motifs of Art Deco, and of technology, together. The mural shows workers building the Chrysler Building, and it also shows an airplane, as well as workers on the assembly line at the Chrysler automobile factory.

There are thirty elevators in the Chrysler Building. The door of each one is made of rare kinds of wood from around the world, inlaid to create variations of a geometric pattern surrounding a lotus flower. The insides of the elevators are similarly decorated.

From the lobby there are two stairways leading down to a level of shops and an entrance to the subway, and also one flight up to

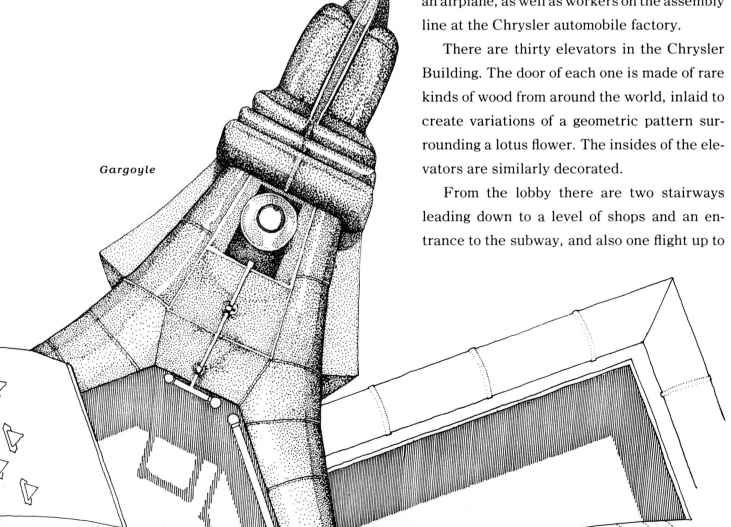

Gargoyle

the first floor of offices. The walls of the stairways are covered with shiny black marble, and the railings are a zigzag pattern of polished steel. In each stairway there are chandeliers made of etched glass in a stainless steel frame, cut in a beveled pattern that sends light shimmering against the dark walls.

Everything about the way the building was constructed, the materials used and the designs and innovations, is a demonstration of the power of man and machines working together, and, of course, an advertisement for Walter Chrysler's products. Particularly noteworthy from an engineering point of view are such modern technical conveniences as a central vacuum-cleaning system and wiring ducts for the telephone and electrical systems underneath the floors. Heating and air conditioning can be controlled from each radiator throughout the building.

When it was built, the Chrysler Building was one of the most elegant office buildings in the city. On the top floor, Walter Chrysler built an exclusive, private club for himself and his executives, called the Cloud Club. There were dining rooms, an old-fashioned tavern, meeting rooms, a library, and a health club. The ceiling was painted with white clouds, and on the walls there was a mural of lower Manhattan. (After Chrysler's offices moved out of the building in the 1950s, the Cloud Club became a public restaurant, which closed in 1979.) Below the Cloud Club was an Observation Level where visitors could pay fifty cents to see a fifty-mile view. In addition to Chrysler, the original tenants of the building included Time, Inc., the American Automobile Association, the Texas Company (now Texaco), and the national Tom Thumb Gold Association.

In time, however, the eye of fashion moved elsewhere. With the building boom of the 1960s, an entirely new style of architecture became popular. Instead of brick buildings, architects designed glass towers like the ones along Park Avenue between 45th and 50th streets (see pages 146–50). The Art Deco elegance of the Chrysler Building began to fade, and tenants moved out. Soon the cost of maintaining the building was greater than income from the rents collected. The building started to have problems.

Luckily, there were those who thought that this historic gem should not be allowed to crumble. In 1975, Massachusetts Mutual Life Insurance Company bought the building for thirty-four million dollars and started a twenty-three-million-dollar renovation project. The building needed a lot of work. The spire had huge leaks in it, the boiler was broken (it kept the temperature at 104 degrees year-round), and the basement was filled with twelve hundred cubic yards of trash.

Four years later, in 1979, the Chrysler Building was bought by Jack Kent Cooke, the owner of the Washington Redskins football team, for ninety million dollars. He continued the renovations, and now the building has been restored to its original glory. By the 1980s, its marvelous design details combined with its attractive lease rates to lure businesses once again. Today, the building's prime tenant is Backer Spielvogel Bates Worldwide, Inc., one of the world's largest advertising and marketing communication companies. The spire is lit every evening from dusk until 2:00 A.M., and the Chrysler Building is not only one of the most familiar, but also one of the best-loved, landmarks in New York City.

Rockefeller Center

1931–1939

*Radio City
Music Hall*

Rockefeller Center is nineteen buildings situated on twenty-two acres in the center of Manhattan: a genuine "city within a city." Covering six city blocks, it has its own intricate network of underground roadways and garages for trucks and automobiles, a web of walkways, fifteen million square feet of rentable office space, more than fifty stores, and thirty restaurants. It is New York's finest achievement in contemporary **urban planning**.

Known by many for its ice-skating rink and its enormous Christmas tree, Rockefeller Center is also the location of the celebrated Rainbow Room, an elegant restaurant and ballroom where you can imagine Ginger Rogers and Fred Astaire swirling across the revolving dance floor sixty-five stories above the glittering city; and Radio City Music Hall, home of the world-famous, high-kicking Rockettes. There is also a business side to Rockefeller Center. It houses some of the most influential media companies in the world—NBC, Time Warner Inc., and the Associated Press—as well as Manufacturers Hanover Trust, the consulates of nine countries, and hundreds of other retail and service businesses. At Rockefeller Center, you can plan a trip, get a United States passport, pick up a book to read on your journey (even one in a foreign language), have your hair cut, and buy a whole new wardrobe. You can see a show or work out at a health club. And in the office buildings, you know that movie contracts are being signed, breaking news is being reported, and financial transactions are taking place.

The galvanizing spirit behind this enterprise was John D. Rockefeller, Jr. The son of the president of Standard Oil Company, the largest oil company in America at the turn of the century, Rockefeller was committed to using his vast resources to promote social, economic, and political reform through **philanthropy**. The projects he helped to finance include, among many, New York's Riverside Church on Riverside Drive and 121st Street; Fort Tryon Park at the northern tip of Manhattan; the Cloisters, the only branch museum of the Metropolitan Museum of Art (see pages 74–85), in the park; and the restoration of Versailles, King Louis XIV's palace near Paris, France. Rockefeller Center, a commercial venture, was his largest undertaking, and it did not begin auspiciously.

The Rockefeller Center story begins in 1926, when the board of directors of the Metropolitan Opera Company began to look for a site for a new opera house. The old Metropolitan Opera House at 39th Street and Broadway (since demolished) had become cramped and run-down, and the streets around it were often clogged with traffic. The opera board set its sights on a piece of land that stretched from 48th to 51st Street, between Fifth Avenue and Sixth Avenue.

The area had once been the site of the Elgin Botanic Gardens, owned by Dr. David Hosack, a Columbia College professor of botany and medicine. Before Hosack took it over, it had been part of Manhattan's "common lands"— owned by the people of the city. (Hosack had achieved renown as the physician who tried to save Alexander Hamilton's life after his fatal duel with Aaron Burr in 1804.)

While Hosack originally leased the land for only five thousand dollars, he ended up investing a considerable amount in the creation and upkeep of the gardens. Eventually, in 1811, he sold the land to New York State at a loss, for seventy-five thousand dollars. Three years later, the state gave the land to Columbia College (chartered in 1754 as King's College) in compensation for some upstate land taken from the college. The college leased the land to a farmer, who paid $125 per year in 1823.

More than one hundred years later, when the Metropolitan Opera board chose the site for a new opera house, it still belonged to Columbia University. The board's consulting architect, Benjamin Wistar Morris, a popular architect who was responsible for the Cunard Building at 25 Broadway, envisioned an entire complex, with the opera house a centerpiece surrounded by tall commercial buildings, elegant shops, gardens, parking garages, and underground passages for pedestrians. The board liked the idea but knew that such an ambitious plan would require strong financial backing.

John D. Rockefeller, Jr., did not regularly attend the opera. Nor did he move in the same social circles as the opera's patrons. But the opera board saw in this wealthy man a new, untapped source of funding and leadership. In addition, Rockefeller's family owned property in midtown—he, his father, and one of his sisters all had houses in the area between Fifth Avenue and Sixth Avenue and 53rd and 54th streets. So they thought he might be interested in such a lofty enhancement to his own neighborhood.

Rockefeller agreed to support the project. In 1928 he leased the property from Columbia University. At that time, the university had been receiving rent of $300,000 per year for the run-down **row houses** in the area—a far cry from the $125 paid by the farmer in 1823, but still far below what the land was worth. Rockefeller's lease agreement for the next fifty years

was for $3.6 to $3.8 million per year.

A year after Rockefeller signed the lease, however, the opera board withdrew from the project. The **stock** market had crashed and the Great Depression of 1929 had begun. The board apparently decided it could not afford such an undertaking. In addition, there had been disagreements about the management of the operation. Rockefeller, holding the lease, had to go ahead without the opera. He would now have to create a vast real-estate development whose purpose would be strictly commercial rather than cultural. (The Metropolitan Opera remained in the old house until 1966, when it finally moved to a newly built opera house at Lincoln Center for the Performing Arts, another Rockefeller-engendered real-estate project, which broke ground in 1959 and became the pioneering and premier cultural complex in the United States.)

By 1930, almost seven million people lived in New York City. They needed space to live and to work, and **real-estate developers** had begun to build massive projects of many tall buildings grouped together to accommodate all of these people: such complexes were a new feature of urban life. Whether we feel ennobled or diminished by such places is largely determined by how well they are designed, how comfortable they are to travel to and through, and whether the streets and spaces around them meet our needs, not only for light and air, but for a sense of both human community and visual delight.

To design Rockefeller Center, John D. Rockefeller, Jr., assembled a distinguished team of architects under the direction of John R. Todd, a senior real-estate and management expert who had been a consultant in 1928 on another Rockefeller project, the restoration and reconstruction of the colonial town of Williamsburg, Virginia. Todd, the son of a midwestern Presbyterian minister, had come to New York for a law degree, and after becoming a lawyer had gone into construction and real estate. Todd's midtown Manhattan projects included the Barclay Hotel, at 111 East 48th Street, and 379 and 385 Madison Avenue, buildings near Grand Central Station.

Todd's team, which came to be called the

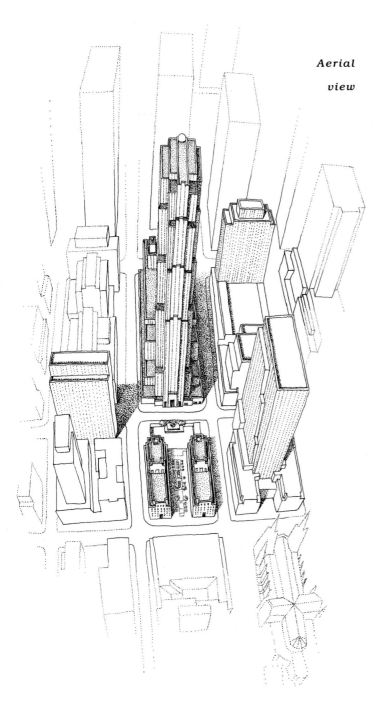

Aerial

view

"Associated Architects," was well rounded. Henry Hofmeister and L. Andrew Reinhard were young, both in their late thirties, and relatively unknown. They had formed their own partnership, Reinhard and Hofmeister, after working for Todd's construction company. Raymond Hood of Hood & Fouilhoux, ten years older, had won the prestigious **design competition** for the Chicago Tribune Tower in 1922, and had designed the American Radiator Building (now the American Standard Building), a widely admired, designated-landmark **skyscraper** at 40 West 40th Street, built in 1923–24 of black brick with **terra-cotta** accents. Harvey Corbett of Corbett, Harrison & MacMurray was a contemporary of Hood's and a respected architect with visionary ideas—he had worked as a consultant to the Regional Plan Association and had pushed for the construction of a tunnel connecting midtown Manhattan to New Jersey before the Holland Tunnel was begun in 1919. Wallace Harrison, Corbett's junior partner and, in his early thirties the youngest member of the team, was distantly related to the Rockefellers by marriage (his wife's brother was married to John D. Rockefeller's only daughter). Later, Harrison, who undertook many projects for the family, created the **master plan** for Lincoln Center for the Performing Arts.

The architects proposed a variety of **plans** for the complex, all of which had in common one important design theme that ensured its success. Given that Rockefeller Center is a monument of modern architecture and twentieth-century building **technology** and **urban planning**, you may be surprised to discover that this theme came directly out of the Ecole des Beaux-Arts training of three of the

Channel

Gardens

principal architects: Hood, Corbett, and Harrison. We have already seen in this book that **Beaux Arts Classicism** emphasized **symmetry**. In groupings of buildings, it called for a balance of forms along sight lines, or **axes**. From the very beginning of the project, it was clear to the architects that the complex would require a main axis to draw the pedestrian—and the eye—from populous Fifth Avenue west toward Sixth Avenue, and that the opera house with its square would be its focal point. When the opera withdrew, an office tower—30 Rockefeller Plaza (formerly called the RCA Building, now the GE Building)—took its place, but the design remained the same. A second axis, a private street running north-south between Fifth Avenue and Sixth Avenue, gives the complex a feeling of separateness from the regimented streets of this part of the city.

The second factor that influenced the successful design of the complex was the city's **zoning** laws. Instead of building uniformly high buildings with large **setbacks**, like the Chrysler Building, the architects decided to distribute the allowable floor space over five towers and a number of lower buildings. The variety of building heights adds immeasurably to the liveliness of the complex.

The fourteen original buildings went up in a burst of construction between 1931 and 1939 that provided jobs for 225,000 workers during the Depression. Their centerpiece is the seventy-story 30 Rockefeller Plaza (constructed in 1931–33). The building's exterior is plain, with gray walls of Indiana **limestone** and windows with aluminum **spandrels** creating long vertical lines up to the flat roof. (This style can also be seen on another celebrated designated landmark: the Empire State Building at 350 Fifth Avenue.) Where the building meets the ground is a four-foot-high band of darker Deer Island **granite**. From the front, the slender building looks like an elongated **spire**, an effect enhanced by three narrow setbacks whose purpose is purely to add a sense of drama to the **facade**.

The grand entrance to 30 Rockefeller Plaza is from Fifth Avenue, down the main axis of the Channel Gardens, amusingly named for the English Channel because they separate the British Building and the Maison Française (or French Building). These are low buildings of nine stories, with the top two floors set back. The horizontal **moldings** above their ground floors and the **cornices** above the sixth and seventh stories, along with the reflecting pools in the gardens, draw the eye to the central sunken plaza and the focal point of 30 Rockefeller Plaza behind it. The consistency of color and shape and attention to the space around the buildings is important to the successful design of Rockefeller Center and ensures that the complex is not just a random jumble of buildings, like many other city blocks.

Nor would it be as chaotic as the surrounding blocks. Although planned when the automobile was still relatively new—in 1929, when the design team got to work, Ford's mass-produced Model T was barely fifteen years old—Rockefeller Center anticipated one of the main problems of the modern city: traffic. Not

only did Rockefeller Center have the first parking garage in an office building in New York City, it also kept freight trucks off the streets with underground ramps for unloading as well as subbasement storage facilities. This underground system keeps trucks from clogging the surrounding streets. The one thousand trucks that daily serve the complex, if parked bumper to bumper on Fifth Avenue, would reach from 42nd Street all the way up to 120th Street—roughly four miles. Imagine the confusion, not to mention the honking horns! Instead, the trucks are thirty feet underground, maneuvering along a network of ramps and loading docks equipped with lifts and truck turntables. Picture a huge freight truck being gently rotated as if it were on the turntable of a record player.

Landscaping and works of art serve to make Rockefeller Center a more hospitable and welcoming place to work or visit. One-quarter of the area occupied by the complex is open space, with gardens and **promenades**, outdoor eating areas and fountains. There are six formal gardens and two acres of landscaped rooftops. Each year, more than twenty thousand plants and flowers bloom, from lilies in the springtime to chrysanthemums in the fall.

Rockefeller also commissioned more than one hundred **murals** and sculptures to decorate the complex. The theme of New Frontiers was chosen, reflecting the pioneering image that Rockefeller Center sought to project, although it is likely that people simply enjoy the art for its own sake. For example, in the reflecting pools of the Channel Gardens are six bronze **fountainheads** in the form of **mythological** Tritons and Nereids, sea creatures that served Poseidon, the Greek god of the sea. The figures are titled *Leadership, Will, Thought, Imagina-*

tion, Energy, and *Alertness,* and were no doubt named to inspire visitors to reflect upon these virtues, as well as to remind them of the founding principles of Rockefeller Center. Created by René Chambellan, they were installed in May, 1935.

The center's most widely known works of art are the two Titans. One is Paul Manship's *Prometheus,* the mythological Greek hero who stole the secret of fire from the gods and shared it with humankind. Prometheus's feat is described by the Greek dramatist Aeschylus, whose words are inscribed on the red Balmoral granite wall behind the sculpture: "Prometheus, teacher in every art, brought the fire that hath proved to mortals a means to mighty ends." (Aeschylus wrote those words in the fifth century B.C. to describe a hero who is often considered a symbol of justice because he gave humans important power that the gods had re-

fused to share.) The bronze figure, covered with **gold leaf**, looks as if it is floating in the air: *Prometheus* is lifted eighteen feet, on a mountain-shaped pedestal representing the earth, and is encircled by a ring with the signs of the **zodiac** to represent the heavens.

Prometheus presides over the sunken plaza, one of the most famous areas in all of New York. An open-air rectangle in the heart of the center, the plaza is known for its resplendent Christmas tree, the lighting of which marks the beginning of the holiday season in the city. In the winter the lower plaza is a skating rink, and in the summer it is an outdoor dining area. At any time of the year, visitors are drawn to the activity in this inviting place—to observe the ice skaters beneath the towering holiday tree, or to stroll among the plants and flowers near the fountain that gushes beneath *Prometheus.*

The other Titan is Lee Lawrie's noted

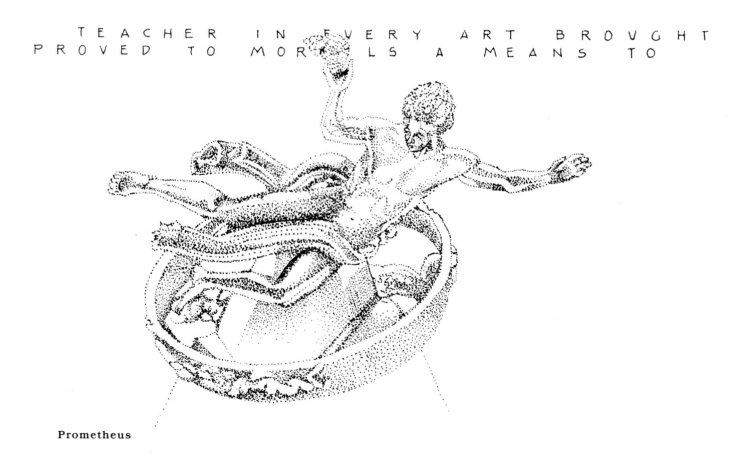

Prometheus

bronze statue of *Atlas,* holding up the world. Lawrie was a student of the celebrated sculptor Augustus St. Gaudens, who was known for his public monuments, such as the recently restored sculpture of General William T. Sherman at the 58th Street and Fifth Avenue entrance to Central Park. *Atlas* was installed in January, 1937, at the entrance of the International Building at 630 Fifth Avenue. It is fifteen feet high and weighs seven tons. *Atlas* emphasizes the stability of the world, with its axis pointing to the North Star. The sculpture reflects the proportion and harmony that Rockefeller Center sought to embody.

Another Lawrie sculpture is *Wisdom,* installed in 1933 over the main entrance to 30 Rockefeller Plaza. Carved stone and cast glass depict the godlike figure of Wisdom, who holds a compass pointing to a square of wavy glass beneath him. The glass, along with panels of limestone to the right and left of the figure, represent important forces in the universe: light and sound.

The works of art commissioned for Rockefeller Center represented a wide range of materials and styles. While the results of the art program are for the most part first-rate, the undertaking was not without its difficulties. For example, for the lobby of 30 Rockefeller Plaza, Mrs. John D. Rockefeller, Jr., and her son Nelson wanted to award a mural commission to the Mexican painter Diego Rivera. After submitting a sketch that showed American scenes, Rivera was told to proceed. When he was almost finished, he added a portrait of the Russian revolutionary leader Vladimir Lenin. Since the United States and the Soviet Union were then ideological enemies, and since the Rockefeller family had earned its fortune

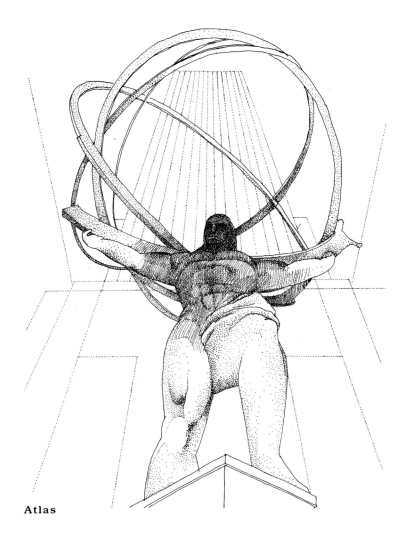

Atlas

through capitalism, it is not altogether surprising that the directors of Rockefeller Center were very upset. Nelson Rockefeller tried to convince Rivera to change the mural, but the artist refused, and was eventually paid his full fee of $22,500. The mural, however, was destroyed, to the dismay of some artlovers; and the Spanish architect and artist José Maria Sert painted American scenes in its place.

Sert's mural, *American Progress,* shows the cooperation of two forces: brain and brawn. On one side of the painting are workers, men of action, and on the other, looking to the sky, are three of the Muses: Poetry, Music, and Dance. In the background are the towers of Rockefeller Center. This juxtaposition is meant to sym-

WISDOM AND KNOWLEDGE SHALL BE THE STABILITY OF THY TIMES

30

Wisdom

bolize the unity of work and ideas. Without one, the other is meaningless. And the labor that created Rockefeller Center would have been for naught without the vision behind it.

In addition to providing a public place for works of art, Rockefeller Center made remarkable contributions to the vitality of New York's tourism and entertainment industry. Radio City Music Hall, the famous 6,200-seat live-entertainment hall on Sixth Avenue, flanking 30 Rockefeller Plaza, was the inspiration of Samuel (Roxy) Rothafel. Roxy was a nationally known producer of radio programs and stage extravaganzas, famous for his motion picture theaters that combined films and **vaudeville** acts. Radio City bears witness to his taste for grandiose and **ornate** construction. The decoration of the hall was overseen by architect/designer Donald Deskey, who had studied at the Art Institute of Chicago and the Ecole de la Grand Chaumière in Paris. Deskey's opulent and flamboyant **Art Deco** design complemented Radio City's enormous theater, with its movable stage and giant organ.

Over the years, Radio City Music Hall has had difficulty turning a profit, and in 1978, the Rockefeller Center management proposed tearing it down to construct a potentially more profitable building on the site. However, because the building had landmark status, the management was required to file an application with the New York City Department of Buildings and the New York City Landmarks Preservation Commission before making any changes.

The public outcry was resounding when the plans to destroy Radio City were revealed, and the New York State Urban Development Corporation responded by proposing several different real-estate ventures to Rockefeller Center management that would help them to make ends meet. One of the proposals, which was never carried out, was to construct an office building on top of the structure. By 1979, Rockefeller Center officials relented and announced that Radio City would remain open, but with a greater variety of entertainment than before.

In times past, Radio City Music Hall introduced current movies with elaborate stage shows featuring the world-renowned Rockettes. Today, the hall is often used for rock concerts and other musical events that bring high ticket prices. However, Radio City Music Hall still mounts extravagant pageants and the Rockettes still perform in them, with their sparkling costumes, synchronized dancing, and high-kick chorus line.

The glamorous Rainbow Room atop 30 Rockefeller Plaza is also as lively as it was when the center first opened. Architect Hugh Hardy was in charge of a successful interpretive restoration of the Rainbow Room in 1987. In the tradition of Rockefeller Center, contemporary works of art were commissioned for the space, including a remarkable wall frieze of hand-blown abstract organic glass forms by glass artist Dale Chihuly.

Rockefeller Center is an important landmark for New York, not just for the beauty of its design—incorporating gardens and open spaces with a unified ensemble of buildings—but also for its contribution to the vitality of midtown Manhattan. It set the standard for other urban complexes and, as the great French architect Le Corbusier put it, "launched [architects] on the paths of the modern spirit."

Lever House

1950–1952

Seagram Building

1956–1958

Perhaps even more symbolic of today's New York City than the great urban complex is the unadorned **skyscraper**. We have already explored the Chrysler Building (see pages 126–33), an older skyscraper that is as handsomely ornamented as any fine example of **Beaux Arts Classicism** from the late nineteenth century. But how do we respond to more recent skyscrapers, the "glass boxes" of modern architecture? Why is it that one may excite us, communicating design perfection and dignity, while another may dull, and even offend, our senses? Can most of us feel much more than discouragement, standing at the foot of a clifflike expanse of metal and glass that rises straight up for thirty stories or more? Two buildings that suggest that modern skyscrapers need not be dehumanizing, and, in fact, that they can be inspiring, are Lever House, 390 Park Avenue, and the Seagram Building, 375 Park Avenue, completed within six years of one another catercorner on Park Avenue and 53rd Street.

Lever House, a twenty-four-story office building of glass and **stainless steel** built in 1950–52, has been called the first modern office tower. Designed by Gordon Bunshaft of Skidmore, Owings & Merrill, it established the modern form for the skyscraper and set the standard for steel-and-glass skyscraper construction in the last half of the twentieth century. Lever House represents the culmination of a century of work in tall building construction.

A skyscraper is a very tall building with a metal framework. Before the use of iron and steel, the only way to build tall buildings of **masonry** was to make the walls of the lower stories very thick, so that they could support the weight of the building. A building whose weight is supported by the walls is said to have **load-bearing walls**. (An exterior wall that does not have a structural purpose is called a **curtain wall**.) There is a limit to how tall a masonry building can be, because the taller it is, the thicker the walls need to be.

Some of these limits were overcome with the use of **cast-iron** construction in the middle of the nineteenth century, as we have seen in our discussion of the E. V. Haughwout Building (see pages 46–53). The exteriors of some

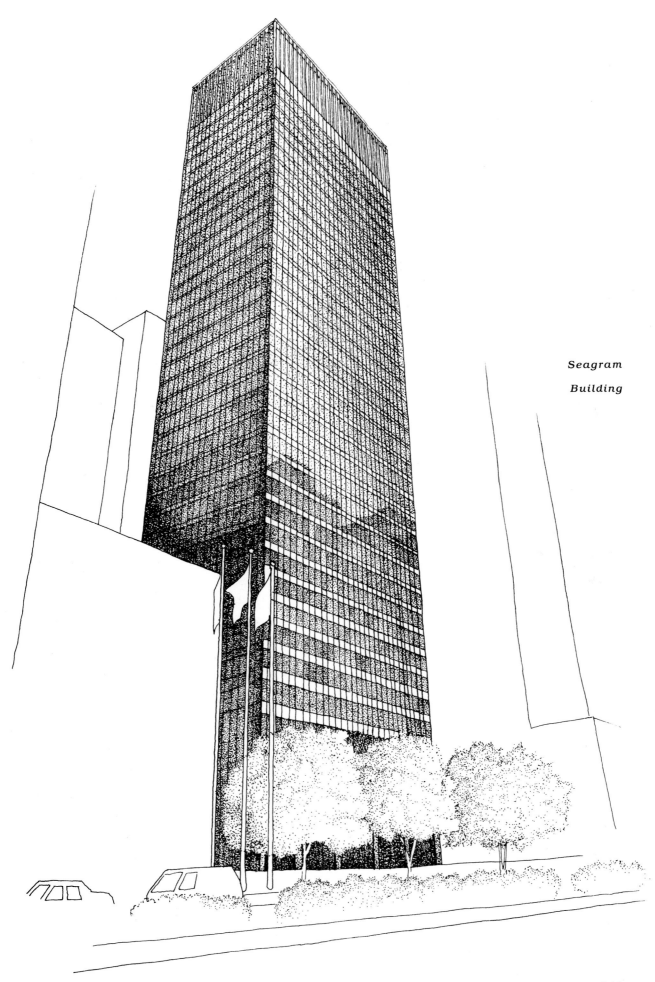

Seagram

Building

143

early **cast-iron buildings** resembled the exteriors of some modern twentieth-century skyscrapers, which also have simple **facades** that reveal the underlying pattern of supports and **beams**. And because the weight of these buildings was supported in part by their metal fronts, the windows could be made much larger than in a masonry building, which is another characteristic of the modern skyscraper.

After the use of metal as a structural material for buildings became commonplace, a major limitation to the size of the buildings was eliminated. Another limitation—the greater distances people had to climb as the number of stories in a building increased—was conquered by the elevator. As we have read, by the 1870s New York City was beginning to have what were then called "elevator buildings." These multistory buildings were equipped with elevators, which made the upper-story apartments as desirable as the lower ones. (Eventually they became more desirable, because of their generally better views and protection from street noises.) The elevator buildings were not entirely metal in structure, but they foreshadowed the modern skyscraper with their height and use of elevators.

Additionally, the design of elevator buildings would be echoed by the later skyscrapers. The elevator buildings of Richard Morris Hunt and George B. Post, in particular, used a **tripartite** design that would prove influential, especially Post's Western Union Building (1873–75) and Hunt's Tribune Building (1873–75), both built in Manhattan (and both now demolished). The three parts, starting from the bottom, were the ground floor or the bottom floors treated as a unit, with a **rusticated** surface; the rest of the floors, treated in a unified manner with each one generally given similar construction; and the roof. This organization divided the building into three (with all, or most, of the floors as a single uniform element) and is sometimes compared to a Classical **column**, with its **base** (the ground floor or floors), **shaft** (the rest of the floors), and **capital** (the roof). Many skyscraper designs followed this design principle as the idea extended into the twentieth century. If you look carefully, you will be amazed at how many New York apartment and office buildings have facades that can be divided into three distinct sections. In this book, The Dakota (see pages 86–91) is a good residential example. A very interesting recent example of an office building that demonstrates the principle is the AT&T Building (1978), at 550 Madison Avenue, designed by Philip Johnson and John Burgee.

By the late nineteenth century, all the elements needed to make skyscrapers were in place: the metal skeleton and the use of iron—and, more and more, steel—and glass as significant building materials. They allowed buildings to soar without the bulkiness of masonry construction, while the passenger elevator moved people rapidly and efficiently within buildings. The stimulus for skyscraper construction—the need for increased commercial space in cities where the available land to build on was becoming more and more expensive—arose during the same period.

The first boom of skyscraper construction took place in Chicago in the 1870s and 1880s. Chicago had by 1870 become the mid-continental hub of American industry, with huge quantities of goods shipped through the city by rail, water, and road. In October of 1871 a fire of unknown origin decimated the city. At the

Lever House

plain, unornamented design that emphasized the "bones" of the building. This design principle has been expressed in the phrase "form follows function"—in other words, the building's outside should reflect how it is used and how it is made on the inside. This gradually became a credo of modern architects. But architects who favored a utilitarian style had to struggle against a prevailing idea of the time, which called for concealing the internal uniformity of the structure of the skyscraper beneath the skin of a more traditional kind of building.

There were many ways to carry out this concept of making the skyscraper look like a conventional structure. For example, the building's facade could be decorated with ornamental details borrowed from historical styles. Ornaments reminiscent of Gothic cathedrals could glorify the skyscraper as a "cathedral of commerce," as in the landmark **Gothic Revival Style** Woolworth Building (1913) at 233 Broadway, a 792-foot tower by Cass Gilbert. Or groups of floors could be designed differently from each other, so that the building was divided horizontally, and would therefore be suggestive of the traditional horizontal elements of smaller types of buildings such as houses. The skyscraper—in using elements of smaller building design—would thus appear smaller than it actually was. Another technique was to divide the facades vertically by using elements such as receding or projecting **bays**, to break up the surfaces and reduce the effect of great height that a uniform surface gives. You can see both of these effects in the facades of the landmark Ansonia Hotel at 2101–2119 Broadway, completed in 1904. Here, the surfaces are broken up with numerous horizontal and vertical design elements.

time, two-thirds of Chicago's buildings were wooden. The fire destroyed about eighteen thousand of them and left about ninety thousand people homeless. It raged over a two-thousand-acre area, and to escape the blaze some people had to take refuge in Lake Michigan. After burning for some twenty-seven hours, the fire was extinguished by a rainfall.

Skyscrapers were an obvious answer to the question of how to rebuild Chicago after the fire. They filled the need for quick, inexpensive, and fire-resistant construction techniques that would produce buildings with large amounts of interior space.

The Chicago skyscrapers were often of

The Chicago architect Louis Sullivan was among the critics of these attempts to disguise the nature of the skyscraper. Sullivan was one of the most important members of what was referred to as the Chicago School of architects. He was educated at the Massachusetts Institute of Technology and the Ecole des Beaux-Arts in Paris. As a young architect, Sullivan joined the Chicago firm of Dankmar Adler, first as chief **draftsman** and then, in 1881, as a partner. Adler & Sullivan subsequently became one of the foremost American architectural firms. After the dissolution of the partnership in 1895, Sullivan worked alone, or occasionally in collaboration.

Sullivan's work emphasized that the external form of the building should reflect its internal organization; that the exterior ornamental detail should not obscure the overall structure of the building; and that the soaring quality of the skyscraper should be given priority.

Have you ever seen the twelve-story Bayard-Condict Building (1897–99) at 65–69 Bleecker Street? If you haven't, it is one landmark that you should try to visit. It is the only building that Sullivan completed in New York City. This Bleecker Street skyscraper is a good example of the design principles that Sullivan followed. Its external curtain wall reflects the internal metal framework of the structure. There is relatively little external decoration until the finely crafted **terra-cotta moldings** seem to blossom at the topmost story. And the thin **colonnettes** within the bays accentuate the verticality of the building.

Now, keeping in mind the architectural principles of skyscraper design expressed in Sullivan's Bayard-Condict Building, let's examine the refinement of those principles in de-

signer Gordon Bunshaft's Lever House. Like Sullivan, Bunshaft was educated at the Massachusetts Institute of Technology; and he joined the firm of Skidmore, Owings & Merrill in 1937. Prior to that he had worked with such notable architects as Raymond Loewy and Edward Durrell Stone, also in New York City.

Lever House was created as the corporate headquarters for the Lever Brothers Company, a leading multinational enterprise that manufactures soaps and food products such as Lux soap and Tide detergent. The Lever Brothers management wanted a striking building that would reflect the company's image of cleanliness in modern living. They turned to Skidmore, Owings & Merrill, and its designer Gordon Bunshaft, for a structure designed in the

Lever

House

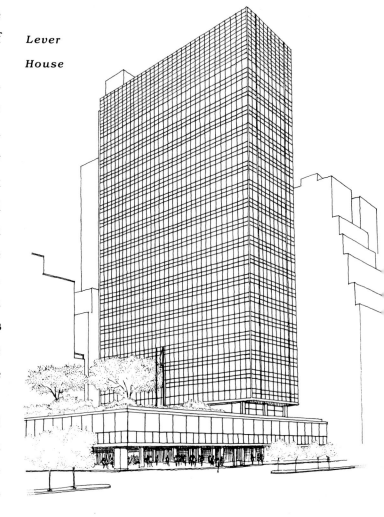

International Style. The International Style was a name created at New York's Museum of Modern Art in 1932, by architecture critic Henry-Russell Hitchcock and Philip Johnson, then director of the museum's department of design and later an important architect. It described a very modern movement in architecture that emphasized airy volume rather than heavy mass; a uniform regularity of design utilizing identical units as opposed to using proportional relations, such as **symmetry**, to organize differing units; and the natural beauty of unadorned building materials instead of surface ornamentation. These principles made it an attractive architectural vision for the Lever Brothers Company.

Lever House's twenty-four stories are clad in glass and stainless steel. The building is basically a vertical slab rising off a horizontal base. The base is set off the ground by square **piers** that allow the ground floor to be used as a garden, which receives light through a hole in the horizontal base. The original design called for an Isamu Noguchi sculpture garden, but it was never built. At the time of his death in 1988, Noguchi was hoping to negotiate with the building's current owner, George Klein, to have it installed, some thirty-five years later.

The vertical slab of the tower is clearly separated from the horizontal base by a single recessed floor. The vertical slab rises uniformly until the top three floors, which are visually differentiated from the others by the use of a horizontal band. In this tripartite division of Lever House (horizontal base, uniform vertical slab, differentiated top three stories) there is a faint echo of the Classical divisions that have already been mentioned: base, shaft, and capital. The vertical slab is of uniform construction un-til the final three floors because internally all those floors serve the same purpose (office space). The top three floors appear different from the other floors externally because they serve a different purpose internally (they house machinery and equipment for the building).

Externally, Lever House avoids the ornamentation that would disguise and break up its uniformity. The exterior is a grid pattern of stainless-steel **mullions** (which are anchored to the building's structural skeleton) and glass panels. The panels come in two different sizes: green-tinted windows and smaller double bands of blue-green glass that are a horizontal counterpoint for the mullions. The result of the use of these materials is that Lever House is reflective during the day (almost every photograph of the building shows the surrounding buildings reflected in its surface) and transparent at night. The lack of external ornamentation allows the essential soaring quality of the skyscraper to come through, making the building look every bit as tall as it actually is, and disguising its great bulk.

Lever House itself provides an important demonstration of the nature of Lever Brothers Company products. The fixed windows of the building can be cleaned only from the outside. Therefore, the architects designed a little gondola car that runs on tracks so that the workers can reach the windows in order to clean them. The cleaning products used are Lever brands, and the sparkling windows of the building are a gigantic advertisement for the company.

The vertical slab of Lever House is only fifty-three feet wide on the Park Avenue side. Because this size tower uses only 25 percent of the total lot area permitted by the **zoning** laws, it was not required to be built with **set-**

backs. This sacrifice of commercial space in order to have a uniform tower shape represented a radical departure from the building priorities of most New York **real-estate developers**.

Bunshaft's Lever House forced architects to rethink the principles of skyscraper design, and many imitations of the building were created. Sometimes, however, other architects' application of the ideas used to build Lever House—the lack of exterior ornamentation, the uniform shape of the tower, and the emphasis on the function of the building dictating the form it would take—resulted in shoddy, imitative buildings. Bunshaft's work became an excuse for ugly, cheap, unornamented skyscrapers. It was also the first of many similar corporate skyscrapers that have changed midtown Manhattan, and especially Park Avenue

and Sixth Avenue, in the past forty years. Almost all of these buildings traded setbacks for street-level open plazas (a revision of the zoning law in 1961, inspired by the Seagram Building, permitted a builder to increase the size of the building in exchange for the provision of a public plaza), which some people use when the weather is nice for resting or eating lunch, but others find uninspiring and dull.

On the other hand, the quality and opulence of Ludwig Mies van der Rohe's Seagram Building at 375 Park Avenue, diagonally across from Lever House and built in 1956–58, provides an example of the successful refinement of Bunshaft's design features.

Like Lever House, the Seagram Building was the result of a corporation's use of architectural **patronage** to enhance its public image. Samuel Bronfman's Joseph Seagram & Sons

Plaza,
Seagram Building

was a major distiller of liquor, and after the repeal of Prohibition in 1933, he began to plan for a headquarters building in Manhattan. The German-born Mies van der Rohe (or Mies, as he was called) was one of the most influential architects of the twentieth century, famous for both the purity and simplicity of his designs and the high level of craftsmanship and materials he insisted upon using. He was awarded the commission to design the Seagram Building after an extensive search for an architect had been made by the company. Phyllis Lambert, Bronfman's architecturally trained daughter, persuaded her father to reject what she felt were the rather ordinary designs that other architects submitted, in favor of the innovative work of Mies. Bronfman named Lambert director of planning for the project.

The result was a spare, dark skyscraper of opulent materials that was recessed dramatically back—one hundred feet—from Park Avenue. The tower, raised on stilts, rises thirty-eight stories above the plaza, over a recessed, glass-enclosed lobby. The shaft is crowned by a simple grid concealing the building's mechanics. The building's steel frame is clothed by a curtain wall of bronze and pink-gray tinted glass, which gives the facade a richness associated with older, beaux-arts buildings. The plaza is equally luxurious: it is made of pink **granite** that is framed on each end of the slab by long parapets of **verde antique**.

The interior of the Seagram Building's office spaces utilized an innovative **modular** system that integrated partitions and lighting for maximum flexibility and convenience in laying out each floor. Interestingly, this modular system is a logical extension of the principle of prefab-

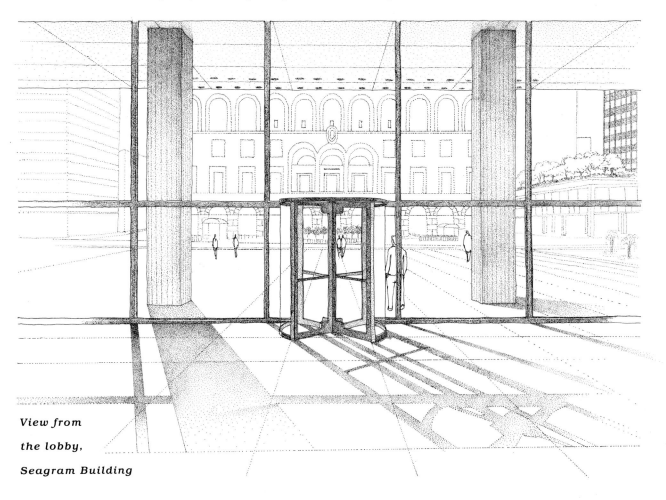

View from the lobby, Seagram Building

ricated parts that made the cast-iron building possible: each module includes the same elements, which can be rearranged to suit the needs of a particular tenant. To preserve the uniformity of the appearance of the windows from the street, Mies built in special venetian blinds for all tenants to use. He designed much of the hardware used in the building, as well as the furniture used for Seagram's own offices, just as Carrère & Hastings had done for the New York Public Library (see pages 98–107), and for the same reason: to ensure that no detail detracted from the overall design.

The building is further marked by the presence of the Four Seasons Restaurant, designed by the distinguished architect Philip Johnson in 1959. Johnson gave the large public space of the restaurant an opulent decor that echoed the design of the Seagram Building itself. One of the dining rooms has a lighted pool at its center, and the walls of the spacious rooms have rich wood paneling. Giant windows stretch from the floor to the ceiling. No matter how creative, or careful, an architect may be, sometimes a design assumes characteristics that were not intended, with striking results: these windows have metallic chain "curtains" that—through a happy accident—ripple pleasingly when the ventilation system is operating.

Mies is famous for saying that, in architecture, "less is more." If you look at the Seagram Building (which was sold in 1980 to the Teachers Investment & Annuity Association), you can begin to see what he meant. It may not be New York's friendliest building, and even on a sunny day you will find its plaza—where monumental works of sculpture are exhibited from time to time—almost deserted, in contrast to the bustle of nearby Rockefeller Plaza (see pages 134–145). But there are many who believe it is a perfect expression of its period. It is worth a visit to see if you agree.

The Seagram Building, completed in 1958, is one of the most recently constructed to be designated a landmark. As you look around the city, see if you can identify even newer buildings that you think will be landmarks of tomorrow. A list of such special places might include Samuel Paley Plaza (1967), a tiny park on East 53rd Street off Fifth Avenue; or Lincoln Center for the Performing Arts (1962–68) between Columbus Avenue and Amsterdam Avenue from West 62nd to West 66th Street, where some of the world's greatest musicians, singers, dancers, and actors perform; or Battery Park City at the southern tip of Manhattan, where a whole new complex of apartment houses, shops, office buildings, public spaces for entertainment, and a school, designed by various architects, is being built since 1980. What about Marcel Breuer's Whitney Museum of American Art (1966) at 945 Madison Avenue, or the spectacular mosaic bench made by community artists that winds around Grant's Tomb at Riverside Drive on West 122nd Street? Or the commanding Jacob K. Javits Convention Center (1979–86), which reclaimed twenty-one acres between Eleventh Avenue and Twelfth Avenue from 34th to 39th Street and was designed by Pei Cobb Freed & Partners? Look at the pale yellow double town house designed by H. Page Cross for Paul Mellon at 125 East 70th Street, which looks as if it was part of our architectural heritage, although it was built in 1965. Could these be designated as landmarks in the future? Maybe there's a place that hasn't even been built yet, that you will discover someday.

Glossary

abutment A part of a structure, such as a bridge, designed with the sole purpose of bearing weight. In a suspension bridge, the anchorage for the cables.

acoustics The conditions of an environment, such as an auditorium, that determine the quality of sound experienced in it.

air rights The property right to the space above ground property. The owner of ground property may, if zoning or other laws permit, sell or lease the air rights above it.

allegory A description or representation of something that is symbolic rather than explanatory. In poetry, for example, a rose can be used as an allegory for beauty.

amateur Someone who pursues an activity, such as collecting art, purely out of personal interest, and not for profit or as a career.

anchorage A masonry vault in which the cables of a suspension bridge are anchored.

antiquities Objects of historical and aesthetic value that have been preserved from ancient times.

aqueduct A channel that carries flowing water. Usually, an aqueduct is part of a water supply system for a city or town.

arcade A covered walkway made up of a series of arches that can be freestanding or a part of a building.

arch An architectural element that is usually curved and composed of wedge-shaped blocks called voussoirs. Arches are often used as frames for doorways, windows, and walkways.

archives A place where documents are preserved for their historical value.

Art Deco A style of architecture, interior decoration, and design that was popular in Europe and America in the 1920s and 1930s. The name Art Deco is derived from the Exposition Internationale des Arts Décoratifs et Industriels Moderne, held in Paris in 1925.

artifact A man-made object, usually from the distant past but not necessarily. Artifacts help archaeologists and historians understand other or earlier cultures.

axis (plural, **axes**) A straight central line, visible or imaginary, that serves as a guideline for a structure's orientation.

balcony A platform that projects from a wall. Exterior balconies, which can be found on many types of buildings, give aboveground access to the outdoors. In theaters, interior balconies are used to provide maximum seating within a limited space.

balustrade A low railing system, usually on a balcony, with ornamental balusters, or supports, that hold up a top rail.

bandcourse A band of masonry that runs horizontally across the face of a building as an element of decoration; it may be plain or, more often, richly detailed.

base The wide bottom part of a column, on which the shaft rests.

bay A principal division of the walls or other part of a building.

beam A long piece of wood, stone, or metal used to support the floors or walls of a building.

Beaux Arts Classicism A style of architecture popular in Europe and America from about 1890 to 1915. The name comes from the Ecole des Beaux-Arts in Paris.

bedrock The solid rock that lies beneath the surface layer of soil or other loose materials.

beehive oven A brick oven with a domed roof that is used for baking, usually found near a fireplace.

"bends," the A dangerous medical condition caused by the change in air pressure that occurs when working in deep water. Symptoms range from muscle cramps to paralysis.

bibliophile Someone who loves and/or collects books.

branch library A small, neighborhood library that is part of a large library system.

brownstone A dark brown or reddish brown sandstone, quarried in the eastern United States and commonly used to face row houses. These row houses are often called brownstones because of the use of this material in their construction.

buffet A sideboard or counter used for food arrangements.

bust A sculpture of a person's head and shoulders.

buttress A projecting structure of masonry or wood supporting or giving stability to a wall or building.

cable A flexible wire rope or metal chain of great strength.

caisson A giant inverted "box" designed to create dry space underwater where laborers can work.

capital The topmost section of a column, often decorated in the style of the Classical orders.

cartouche A decorative element that looks like an ornately framed medallion or shield.

cast iron An alloy of iron, carbon, and silicon that is cast in sand molds to produce hard metal products, such as building facades, machine parts, and furniture.

cast-iron building A building with a load-bearing facade made of prefabricated cast-iron parts.

clapboard siding A type of exterior wall surface that uses long horizontal boards. Most wooden houses have this kind of siding.

Classical orders The standardized elements of classical architecture, consisting of three types, from the simplest to the most ornate: the Doric, the Ionic, and the Corinthian.

clerestory In a building, a row of windows in the upper part of a wall that rises above adjacent roofs.

coffer A recessed panel, usually square or octagonal, that is used in decorative ceilings.

colonnette A small column.

colony A land ruled by another country. New York was one of thirteen colonies ruled by England before the American Revolution.

column A cylindrical structure used as an architectural support.

commuter A person who regularly travels between places, such as the city and the suburbs or the countryside.

concourse An open space or hall (such as in a railway terminal) where crowds gather.

Corinthian order See **Classical orders**

cornice A decorative molding, at the top of a structure, that projects outward and serves as a finishing or "crowning" element.

courtyard A roofless enclosure adjacent to or inside a building.

cove lighting Lighting concealed in a trough at the top of a wall.

cresting An ornament on a roof or wall, highly decorative and usually made of iron or other metals.

cross-and-Bible pattern A decorative motif found on wood surfaces such as doors or wall paneling that depicts a cross lying in the center of an open book.

cupola A small, often circular, structure built on top of a roof.

curtain wall An exterior wall that has no load-bearing function.

deck The roadway of a bridge.

design competition An architectural contest in which plans are submitted by entrants and the winner is chosen by judges.

diversity The condition of being different.

dome A hemispherical roof or ceiling.

Doric order See **Classical orders**

dormer A structure that projects from a sloping roof, usually housing a window or a ventilation opening.

draftsman A skilled artist who draws sketches and precise plans of buildings, and parts of buildings.

drawing room A room for relaxing and entertaining guests, equivalent to the living room of today.

drip molding A wide strip of molding situated above a window or doorway, designed to keep rainwater off the wall's surface.

dumbwaiter A small elevator used for transporting food and dishes from one story of a building to another.

Dutch door A door that is divided in half so that the top and bottom can be opened and closed separately.

eclecticism A philosophical approach that is distinguished by its selection of what appears to be the best of different doctrines, methods, or styles.

Ecole des Beaux-Arts The French school of art, located in Paris, that trains artisans and architects.

el An urban mass-transit system that runs on tracks elevated above the ground.

Empire Style A style popular in France during the first Napoleonic Empire, particularly associated with the types of furniture and decoration ordered by the Emperor Napoleon for his residences. The Empire Style was influential throughout Europe and America.

entablature A horizontal beam that is supported by the columns of a structure.

estate The property and/or buildings owned by an individual, family, or institution.

facade The exterior face of a building, often the one that serves as the architectural front.

fanlight A window with a round top and multiple panes of glass that resembles a fan. Such windows are usually seen above a door in the facade of a building.

Federal Style A style of architecture popular in the United States between 1790 and 1830.

finial An ornament that crowns an architectural feature.

floor plan A drawing of the layout of a floor in a building.

foundry A factory where molten metal is cast into various forms.

fountainhead The source of water for a fountain. Many fountainheads are ornamental.

French door A full-length door with rectangular glass panes.

fresco A mural that is painted on wet plaster.

frieze A painted or sculpted decoration that appears in a horizontal format.

gable The vertical triangular end of a building beneath a peaked roof.

Georgian Revival Style A style of architecture popular in the United States between 1890 and 1915 that was inspired by Georgian Style and Federal Style.

Georgian Style A style of architecture popular in England and its North American colonies during the reigns of kings George I, II, and III, from 1714 to 1830. In North America, it was largely replaced by the Federal Style after the Revolution.

gold leaf Gold that is beaten into a very thin sheet so that it can then be used to coat a surface, giving the object the appearance that it is solid gold.

Gothic The architectural style that emerged during the Middle Ages in France, characterized by rich ornamentation and pointed arches, as in cathedrals.

Gothic Revival Style A style of architecture inspired by Gothic architecture popular in the United States between 1820 and 1860.

granite A natural igneous rock notable for its hardness and crystalline appearance. It occurs in pink and gray colors and is often used for monuments.

gridiron Something consisting of, or covered with, a network.

groin The line formed by the intersection of the surfaces of two vaults.

head house A part of a passenger railroad terminal that provides accommodations for people who are waiting for trains.

hearth The stone or masonry floor of a fireplace.

High Victorian Gothic Style A style of architecture popular in the United States between 1860 and 1890, which is distinguished from Gothic Revival Style by a more abundant use of color and ornament.

High Victorian Italianate Style A highly ornamental style popular in the United States between 1860 and 1890, inspired by Italian Renaissance architecture.

infrastructure The underlying foundation or basic structure of a system—for example, of a city.

inlaid wood A piece of wood that has been decorated using the method of inlay. This technique involves the embedding of small pieces of one material into another.

insulation A material or substance that is added to the walls of a building in order to prevent loss of heat or cold.

International Style A modern style of architecture popular between the 1920s and 1960s.

Ionic order See **Classical orders**

isotropic Exhibiting properties with the same values when measured along axes in all directions.

keystone The center, or locking block, of an arch. This stone holds the others in place. Also, any stone in a structure that locks others in place.

layout The arrangement of rooms, doors, windows, and so forth in a building.

lean-to A small extension to a building whose supports lean against the main structure. The roof of a lean-to has only one slope.

limestone A soft, sedimentary rock used in construction, especially for facades and sculpture.

lintel A horizontal beam over an opening that carries the weight of the wall above it.

load-bearing wall A wall that supports an additional structural load as well as its own weight.

loggia A roofed, open gallery, often on the upper stories of a building and overlooking an open court.

mansard A decorative roof with a flat top and steep sloping sides.

mansion A large, sometimes imposing house with many rooms, usually freestanding and surrounded by grounds.

mantel The beam or arch that serves as a support for the masonry section above a fireplace.

marble A hard limestone that shines when polished and is often used as a building material, for its decorative effects, and for sculpture.

masonry Various kinds of stonework used in construction.

master plan A plan that provides overall and long-term guidance for a project.

memorabilia Things that are evocative of a period and worthy of remembrance.

moat Originating in early European history, a broad, deep trench surrounding a building or town and usually filled with water as a defense against intruders.

modular Constructed with standardized units or dimensions for flexibility and variety in use.

molding An ornamental strip of plaster or wood decorating or lining an architectural element, like a wall, ceiling, or doorway.

monitor A raised central portion of a roof having low windows or louvers that provide light and/or air. Similar to a clerestory.

monoliths Large stones that are usually positioned vertically. A column is a monolith when it is carved from a single stone.

motif A dominant theme or element that is often repeated within a story, building, or work of art.

mullion A slender vertical member between units of a window.

mural A painting that is made directly on a wall, thereby becoming a permanent part of it.

mythological Anything that relates to or describes characters and situations from the stories of gods and supernatural beings.

narrative A story that is related with words, pictures, movement, or music.

Neo-Classical Revival Style A style of architecture popular in the United States between 1890 and 1915 that is loosely based upon classical architecture, but does not adhere to its rules.

old master painting A painting produced by one of the great artists of the past five hundred years.

oriel A projecting bay or window, forming the extension of a room, first used in medieval English residential architecture.

ornate Elaborately, and sometimes excessively, decorated and detailed.

outhouse Before modern plumbing, a small building, situated away from other structures and containing a bench with holes, used instead of a toilet.

overmantel A decorative panel that appears over a mantelpiece.

palazzo The Italian word for palace.

parlor A room designated for receiving guests, and usually furnished with formal furniture and a display area for the finer possessions of the inhabitants of the house. Similar to the living room of today.

parquet Flooring composed of short strips of wood, often of contrasting varieties, that form geometric and/or decorative patterns.

party wall A common wall that divides two adjoining properties, such as row houses.

pastoral A word used to describe things that have the simplicity, charm, and other characteristics associated with the countryside.

patron A person who supports the work of an artist or institution with gifts of money and effort.

pavilion A separate or semidetached structure used for specialized activities, such as parties.

pediment An ornament used to designate doorways or windows; usually in a triangular shape, it can be curved as well. In classical architecture, it is the triangular part of the roof, often filled with sculpture.

pewter A metal made from tin and silver; used for many household objects, including tableware.

philanthropy Activities and concerns that are oriented toward the benefit of humankind or specific groups of people.

pier A column designed to support an especially heavy and concentrated load; usually constructed of masonry.

pilaster A decorative feature that imitates and resembles a column but does not support anything.

plan A drawing made to scale to represent the view of a building from above.

pneumatic tube A tube that can be opened at either end that contains compressed air. Objects placed in one end of the tube will be carried to the other end by the force of the compressed air. Often used in large buildings to carry messages contained in "capsules" from one place to another.

porcelain A type of clay used to create ceramics noted for their delicate appearance and translucent quality. Also, the objects made from porcelain.

porch A structure attached to a building, to shelter an entrance or to serve as a semi-enclosed space.

portico A colonnade or covered walk with a roof that is supported by columns; often found at the entrance to a building.

portrait An artist's rendering of the likeness of a person.

prefabrication The practice of manufacturing things such as houses in standardized parts or sections. This method of production makes it possible to offer products that are inexpensive and quick to assemble.

promenade A place where people can go for a leisurely stroll.

provenance A place or source of origin. This word is often used when describing the history of ownership of works of art.

pyramid A triangular structure, originally used as a funerary monument to deceased persons of authority or status in ancient Egypt. The base of the structure is square in plan, with four identical triangular sides that narrow and slope inward toward the top, ending in a single point.

real-estate developer A person who buys property with the intention of being able to make a profit by its sale.

Renaissance The revival of interest in the culture of the classical period that took place in Europe from the fourteenth to the seventeenth century. In architecture, Renaissance style is characterized by classical orders, round arches, and symmetrical composition.

Renaissance Revival Style A style of architecture and design popular in the United States between 1820 and 1860 and inspired by Italian Renaissance buildings.

rendering A formal drawing of a building in perspective that is usually made by an architect for the purpose of presentation to a client.

renovate To restore or repair an already existing building.

rosette A round, decorative ornament that is carved or painted like a rose or flower.

rotunda A round building or part of a building, generally with a domed ceiling.

row house A residential structure that is part of a series of identical houses sharing party walls.

rustic Of or pertaining to things associated with the country, as distinguished from towns or cities.

rusticated A style of masonry that uses blocks of stone with deeply recessed joints and heavy faces. This type of masonry is often used on the basement or ground-floor facade of buildings because it is said to give the impression of strength.

saltbox A wood-frame dwelling with two stories in front and one behind and a roof with a long rear slope.

sandhog A laborer who works, usually in a caisson, at digging underwater tunnels or foundations.

sarcophagus An ornamental stone coffin originating in the cultures of ancient Greece and Rome. Carvings on these coffins were elaborate, and they often depicted the values or accomplishments of the deceased.

sconce A candlestick or light that is attached to a wall bracket.

Second Empire Style A style of architecture popular in the United States between 1860 and 1890, which was inspired by the architecture of Paris in the Second Empire (1852–71). The hallmark of the style is the high, ornate mansard roof.

Second Renaissance Revival A style of architecture and design popular in the United States from 1890 to 1915, which is chiefly distinguished from Renaissance Revival by the larger and more impressive buildings it produced.

setback Placement of the upper stories of a building so as to take up less than the full space covered by the lower stories. Some buildings have several setbacks. Some zoning laws permit buildings with setbacks to have more floors.

shaft The middle section of a column, between the base and the capital.

shrine An object or place devoted to holy relics or of special religious importance. One type of shrine can contain the remains and relics of a saint, while others are simply places of devotion.

sidelight A vertical rectangular window alongside a door, often with panes of colored glass.

siding A material, such as wooden boards or metal pieces, that composes the exposed surfaces of an exterior wall.

sinuous Having many curves, bends, and turns.

skyscraper A very tall, modern building with a steel framework. It is a multistory structure and uses elevators to transport people and goods internally.

spandrel In a multistory building, the area of wall between the top of the window of one story and the sill of the window directly above it. Also, an area or surface, roughly triangular in shape, as below a stair or between two adjoining arches.

speculate To assume a business risk by acquiring such assets as property or stocks in the expectation of profit through a change in their market value.

spire A pointed extension of a building that resembles a tall cone and rises above the roof.

stacks A term used for both the bookshelves and the main area where books are stored or shelved in a library.

stainless steel Steel that has chromium and nickel added to it so that it is especially resistant to rust and corrosion.

steel A metal alloy, combining iron and carbon, but of greater strength than iron.

stock Shares in the ownership of a corporation.

stoop A platform or small porch raised by a few steps that leads up to the main entrance of a building, usually a residence.

streamlined Contoured to reduce resistance to motion through air or water.

stress A force exerted when one element in a structure presses on or twists against another.

stucco A mixture of cement, lime, sand, and water that is applied to walls and dries hard. It can create a rough surface or be molded into fine, smooth shapes.

stud One of the smaller upright boards in the framing of a building to which sheathing, paneling, or laths to hold plaster are fastened.

suspension bridge A type of bridge in which the roadway is suspended in the air by a network of cables or chains anchored by supports at either end.

sweatshop A shop where underpaid workers are employed and where working conditions are often dangerous and unsanitary.

symmetry There are two kinds of symmetry in design. In bilateral symmetry, the parts on both sides of a dividing line are the same in shape, size, or position. In radial symmetry, the object is arranged uniformly around a central point.

technology The branch of knowledge that deals with applied science and engineering.

tenement An urban residential building that meets only the minimum standards of sanitation, safety, and comfort; usually occupied by economically disadvantaged families.

tension The stress resulting from the elongation of an elastic body, such as a bridge girder.

terrace An outdoor raised platform adjoining a building.

terra-cotta A hard, unglazed type of clay; used for ornamental work on exteriors, roofs, and floor tiles.

thatch A plant material (such as straw) used as a sheltering cover, most often for houses.

topography The physical or natural features of an area of land and their structural relationships.

tripartite Divided into three parts.

trundle bed A low bed that is usually on casters so that it can easily be slid under a higher bed.

truss Any of various structural frames based on the geometric rigidity of the triangle. Trusses are frequently seen on bridges.

urban planning The activity or profession of determining the future physical arrangement and condition of a city.

vaudeville A type of theatrical entertainment consisting of a number of individual performances. This form of theater was popular in the United States from the 1880s to the early 1930s.

vault A masonry structure or covering constructed on the principle of the arch.

verde antique A green-veined marble.

vestibule A small room that is usually located at a doorway, leading into a larger space.

villa A large country residential dwelling, meant for relaxation and entertainment in a rural setting.

vista The view of an outdoor scene, usually from a window or a doorway.

wainscot A decorative or protective covering made of wood or plaster, applied to the lower portion of an interior wall.

wrought iron A type of iron that is refined through a repeated process of hammering out impurities.

zodiac Twelve signs associated with astrology that are derived from apparent paths of the principal planets, the sun, and the moon.

zoning Ordinances that divide a city or town into different sections reserved for specific purposes such as businesses, residences, or manufacturing.

Index

Acknowledgments

It's clear that I love New York; its history and buildings, too. So do many others who collaborated on this effort: The Landmarks Preservation Foundation's staff and board, members of the Landmarks Preservation Commission staff; the owners, occupants, and managing agents of landmark buildings; and a wide range of individual and institutional sources that focus on New York City's architecture and history.

My thanks, also, to the following individuals for their help toward the realization of this book—Paul Gottlieb, Carl Spielvogel, Ellen Wasserman, Michelle Hong, Martha Thomas, Rodger Hurley, Danielle Desruisseaux, Deborah Bershad, and Judie Janney; and The Commonwealth Fund for its ongoing support and encouragement.

Space limits the inclusion of the numerous others who shared their time, knowledge, and perspectives. To all who helped, including those whose names might have inadvertently been omitted, I extend my appreciation. Without their invaluable assistance, *Landmarks: Eighteen Wonders of the New York World* would not have been possible.

Barbaralee Diamonstein